MEDIA AND JOURNALISM
PROFESSIONALS

PRACTICAL CAREER GUIDES

Series Editor: Kezia Endsley

Clean Energy Technicians, by Marcia Santore
Computer Game Development & Animation, by Tracy Brown Hamilton
Craft Artists, by Marcia Santore
Criminal Justice Professionals, by Kezia Endsley
Culinary Arts, by Tracy Brown Hamilton
Dental Assistants and Hygienists, by Kezia Endsley
Education Professionals, by Kezia Endsley
Fine Artists, by Marcia Santore
First Responders, by Kezia Endsley
Health and Fitness Professionals, by Kezia Endsley
Information Technology (IT) Professionals, by Erik Dafforn
Mathematicians and Statisticians, by Kezia Endsley
Media and Journalism Professionals, by Tracy Brown Hamilton
Medical Office Professionals, by Marcia Santore
Multimedia and Graphic Designers, by Kezia Endsley
Nursing Professionals, by Kezia Endsley
Plumbers, by Marcia Santore
Skilled Trade Professionals, by Corbin Collins
Veterinarian Technicians and Assistants, by Kezia Endsley

MEDIA AND JOURNALISM PROFESSIONALS

A Practical Career Guide

TRACY BROWN HAMILTON

ROWMAN & LITTLEFIELD
Lanham • Boulder • New York • London

Published by Rowman & Littlefield
An imprint of The Rowman & Littlefield Publishing Group, Inc.
4501 Forbes Boulevard, Suite 200, Lanham, Maryland 20706
www.rowman.com

6 Tinworth Street, London, SE11 5AL, United Kingdom

British Library Cataloguing in Publication Information Available

Library of Congress Cataloging-in-Publication Data

Names: Hamilton, Tracy Brown, author.
Title: Media and journalism professionals : a practical career guide /
  Tracy Brown Hamilton.
Description: Lanham : Rowman & Littlefield, [2021] | Series: Practical
  career guides | Includes bibliographical references. | Summary: "Media
  and Journalism Professionals: A Practical Career Guide includes
  interviews with professionals in a field that has proven to be a stable,
  lucrative, and growing profession"—Provided by publisher.
Identifiers: LCCN 2020052094 (print) | LCCN 2020052095 (ebook) | ISBN
  9781538144794 (paperback) | ISBN 9781538144800 (ebook)
Subjects: LCSH: Mass media—Vocational guidance. | Journalism—Vocational
  guidance.
Classification: LCC P91.6 .H36 2021 (print) | LCC P91.6 (ebook) | DDC
  302.23023—dc23
LC record available at https://lccn.loc.gov/2020052094
LC ebook record available at https://lccn.loc.gov/2020052095

Contents

Introduction

So You Want a Career in Media and Journalism?

Welcome to the world of media and journalism! This book is the ideal start for understanding the various careers available to you within the journalism and media industry, which is right for you, and what path you should follow to ensure you have all the training, education, and experience needed to succeed in your future career goals—as well as advice on how to make contacts, identify stories, and pitch ideas.

The fields of journalism and media are no doubt exciting, challenging, creative, and undeniably interesting—and broad. There are many roles and careers that fall under the umbrella of journalism and media, from writer to editor to photographer and even cartoonist. Having so many paths to choose from is exciting, but it can also make it difficult to choose which is the most fitting for you.

A Career in the Media and Journalism Industry

Journalism and media have historically played an important role in society, and their significance continues around the world today. In the United States, some refer to the journalism and media industries as the "fourth estate," carrying the responsibility of monitoring and playing "watchdog" to the three branches of government: the legislative, executive, and judicial. So being part of the journalism and media profession carries with it a fairly big responsibility.

This book will focus on the most common jobs in media and journalism, including the following:

- Editor in chief
- Editor/senior editor
- Copyeditor
- Proofreader
- Reporter
- Correspondent
- Broadcast journalist
- Photojournalist

And for every one of these jobs, there are people who specialize in a particular subject area (although many journalist and media professionals are generalists). These areas of expertise include anything from politics to economics to sports to fashion.

The book will describe the functions of these jobs, as well as the key differences between them—for example, the difference between a blogger and a columnist. For many of these jobs, the education and experience required for a successful career will be similar if not identical, and this will also be explained in the book.

The Market Today

How does the job market look for young people seeking to enter the field of media and journalism? It is slightly mixed. On one hand, people will always want access to information about what is going on in the world, so reliable, thorough, professionals who research and provide that information to the public will remain in demand. Also, new technologies make it increasingly possible for the public to join the information-gathering and sharing arena, as well as make it possible for news to be shared around the clock via various media.

On the other hand, according to the US Bureau of Labor Statistics (BLS),[1] jobs for reporters and correspondents will decline by 12 percent from 2018 to 2028, and during the same period, jobs for editors will decrease by 3 percent and for photographers decrease by 6 percent. At the same time, universities offering programs in journalism and media studies report a notable increase in applicants[2]—up to 24 percent in some cases—which shows that the future generation is interested in keeping the field alive and thriving.

One reason for the predicted decline is what is called *media conglomeration,* which refers to many smaller media outlets being bunched together under one large company. We will cover this more in chapter 1. Another reason for the decline in the job market is the money previously earned through advertising, particularly in print media, has reduced significantly over the last decade or so, which has drained funding for many publications across the country and world.

Because jobs are scarcer than in previous times, competition is extremely intense, but please don't let this discourage you. This book will give you lots of advice for how to break into the field, such as starting out as an intern or producing content for the Web or wireless communication devices. Working as a freelance reporter or writer is also a great way to launch your career and develop a good portfolio, gain rich experience, and make valuable contacts along the way. Freelancing is also a desirable career on its own, which we will also address later in this book.

A career in the journalism and media industry is an exciting one, offering diverse roles and a chance for continuous learning, as well as a responsibility to deliver news to broad audiences.
SDI PRODUCTIONS/E+/GETTY IMAGES.

It will probably come as no surprise that the best geographical locations in the United States and around the world for launching a successful career in journalism and media are big cities. Do not let this discourage you, though, if you do not live in or have the desire to live in a large metropolitan area. Technology has made it possible to work remotely from anywhere in the country or the world.

However, if you are open to relocating to land your dream job (or even an entry-level internship that may eventually lead to your dream job), FitSmallBusiness[3] published the following rankings of the ten best cities in the United States for careers in journalism and media (note these are specifically for jobs with newspapers, television networks, and radio stations). The data is based on these factors, as quoted in the article:

- **Population (25%):** Larger cities tend to be central hubs for news disseminated on all three media outlets noted above, so we started by finding the top 100 most populous cities in the U.S. This was how we determined what cities we would evaluate using additional, media-specific criteria.
- **Media channels (25%):** The media channels we considered were newspaper, television, and radio; even with the proliferation of digital media, these collectively make up the largest job market for journalists. Predominantly, we used the number of outlets as a means of determining job opportunities.
- **Salary (20%):** We looked at average salaries to determine the potential for earning a decent living. Not only does this indicate possible entry-level wages but also gives journalists a sense of career earning opportunities.
- **Cost of living (15%):** Cost of living naturally offsets salary and determines what kind of life a journalist can afford. We favored lower costs of living as this allows salaries to stretch farther.
- **Colleges & universities (15%):** While the existence of high-ranking journalism schools at local colleges and universities is not a direct indicator of career growth, it does suggest opportunities for internships as well as professional development. Both of these can further a journalist's career.

Here are the cities that made the list, in order of first to tenth:

- New York, New York
- Washington, D.C.
- Los Angeles, California

- Chicago, Illinois
- Boston, Massachusetts
- Philadelphia, Pennsylvania
- Phoenix, Arizona
- San Antonio, Texas
- Dallas, Texas
- Houston, Texas

But again, if you don't live near these cities or don't see yourself wanting to in the future, don't despair: Freelance, contract, and remote opportunities also exist, from the smallest towns to the biggest cities, and all over the world.

> "You need many qualities [in this field] that may seem to be at odds with each other: Very organized but flexible. Tenacious but polite. Focused but nimble. Adaptable but resilient. Open-minded but mission-focused."—C. B. is an equine journalist

What Does This Book Cover?

This book covers the following topics for all the aforementioned careers, as well as others:

- What kind of job best suits your personality and preference for working conditions, hours, educational requirements, work culture, and atmosphere? The book will describe the day-to-day activities involved in each job and what a typical day at work will look like
- How to form a career plan—starting now, wherever you are in your education—and how to start taking the steps that will best lead to success
- Educational requirements and opportunities and how to fulfill them
- Writing your résumé, interviewing, networking, and applying for jobs
- Resources for further information

Once you've read the book, you will be well on your way to understanding what kind of career you want, what you can expect from it, and how to go about planning and beginning your path.

Where Do You Start?

All the jobs we cover in this book require at least a high school degree or equivalent, such as a General Education Development (GED) degree and some on-the-job training. Others require a four-year degree and even a master's degree—and the subjects you can follow will also vary. Communications, politics, writing, economics—journalism and media studies, of course—are all good choices for an educational track leading to a career in journalism and media.

A lot of choosing the right career for you will also depend on your personality and interests outside work—such as whether you work better with people or independently, whether you want to be the boss or work for someone you admire, and what you want your life to include outside working hours—including hobbies and other activities that are important to you, and so on.

After high school, knowing how to choose and apply to vocational training such as an apprenticeship or a college program will be the next step in your path. The information in chapter 3 will help you navigate this important stage and know what questions to ask, how to best submit yourself as a candidate, and the right kinds of communication skills that are key to letting future employers or trainers understand who you are and what your potential is.

Thinking about the future and your profession is exciting and also a bit daunting. With this book, you will be on track for understanding and following the steps to get yourself on the way to a happy and successful future in the journalism and media industry. Let's get started!

Why Choose a Career in Media and Journalism?

*D*o you have a natural curiosity and a desire to develop your understanding of what is going on in the world around you? Are you fascinated by the stories of other people, from politicians to sports stars to everyday heroes, the lives they live, or the things they have accomplished? Are you committed to hearing different sides and points of view of the same issue? A career in journalism and the media will enable you not only to get the "full story" on topics that interest and affect you but also to enable others to have clear access to information that impacts their lives as well.

The fact that you picked this book off the shelf and are reading it indicates that you are ready to take your curiosity, research skills, and talent for storytelling to the next level: considering the journalism and the media as a career. Choosing a career is a difficult task, but as we discuss in more detail in chapter 2, there are many methods and means of support to help you refine your career goal and a profession that will be satisfying and will fit you the best. Of course, the first step is understanding what a particular field—in this case journalism and the media—actually entails and informing yourself on the outlook of the profession. That is the emphasis of this chapter, which looks at defining the field in general and then in more specific terms, as well as examining the past and predicted future of the field.

Journalism and the media as a whole encompass a number of different jobs. Traditionally, one may think of a journalist or media professional as being a person who carries around a small notebook interviewing people to get to the bottom of a story. That is certainly true, but there are other types of careers that fall under the umbrella of media and journalism, such as editors, photographers, cartoonists, radio and television broadcasters, and so on. Beyond that, there are different types of journalism, based on such things as format, subject matter, and the voice of the journalist in the work itself. For example, there is a difference between an opinion piece and a news article in which writers convey facts without revealing their own viewpoints. (There will be a lot more on this in the book.)

What all careers in the field of journalism and the media have in common is storytelling—by which we mean delivering accounts of actual events and not inventing fiction. There are many ways in which people want to learn about what's going on in the world (e.g., television, print media, online news providers, etc.), and journalists and media professionals are responsible for providing these services.

Depending on the media outlet for which you work and the type of story you follow, you could be part of providing anything from live, 24-hour, global news on television or working on longer, more contextual articles for monthly magazines. You may be working on a daily local newspaper or broadcasting live from a glamorous red carpet or a dangerous war zone.

You can say for all areas of journalism and the media, a successful professional will have excellent communication skills, willingness to work outside the 9-to-5 mindset in many cases, and a desire to work with lots of interesting people from various backgrounds, experiences, and points of view. An ability to collaborate and to allow yourself to be "behind the scenes" rather than the front and center of a story is also important.

You should also have a hunger for continuous learning. You will be faced with new facts and information, with new challenges, events, people, and situations constantly in your work. You will also have to keep up with fast-moving technology, including how the news is gathered and delivered. If you are truly passionate about these things, a career in journalism and the media will be continuously satisfying. It is also a competitive field, often demanding long hours working in high-pressure, often stressful environments (with tight deadlines). There are many talented, creative, and motivated people vying for positions in what is one of the most creative and interesting jobs out there.

So as with any career, there are pros and cons. In balancing the good points and less-attractive points of a career, you must ask yourself whether, in the end, the positive outweighs any negatives you may discover. This chapter will also help you decide whether a career in journalism and the media is actually the right choice for you. And if you decide it is, the next chapter will further offer suggestions for how to prepare your career path, including questions to ask yourself and resources to help you determine more specifically what kind of career related to journalism and the media suits you the best.

Types of Journalism

In broad terms, there are many distinct types of journalism, which are defined in the following sections. Deciding on media and journalism certainly narrows the field of career choice considerably, but there are still many decisions to make. For example, what type of journalism do you want to pursue? What subjects do you want to cover, if you choose to be a reporter, and if you choose to be an editor, what kinds of topics do you wish to publish or produce?

Also, which medium is right for you? For example, do you see yourself writing news for the radio or delivering live broadcasts in front of the camera? Depending on your ambitions, your career and education path may differ. Here are the main "types" of journalism, according to Indeed.com.[1]

INVESTIGATIVE JOURNALISM

This type of journalism—perhaps the main one that comes to mind—involves exactly what its name indicates: investigation. Journalists who focus on investigative reporting base their work on extensive research. The task is to probe an issue thoroughly and discover evidence on which to base conclusions expressed in the stories. This type of journalism takes time and preparation to do successfully and honestly. It entails connecting with reliable sources (people who are qualified to provide insight, expertise, and authoritative evidence on a particular subject), preparing, and researching. Investigative journalism can be found in both print and broadcast media.

WATCHDOG JOURNALISM

Watchdog journalists are a type of security guard in the media and journalism world and are tasked with keeping a watchful eye on powerful, influential segments of society (such as government and large corporations). This type of journalism is intended to expose wrongdoings that give an unfair advantage to some while causing harm to the rest of a community. Its focus is on ensuring behaviors of those in power are fair and legal. Watchdog journalism can be found in both print and broadcast media.

ONLINE JOURNALISM

As its name suggests, online journalism is a form that is shared digitally, via online newspapers and magazines and their supporting social media. This content is often available online, but in some cases, subscriptions are required to access stories delivered electronically (such as with the *New York Times*). Online journalism is relatively new and should follow the same practices of traditional print journalism (such as credibility with sources). A strong benefit of online journalism is that stories can be shared quickly as compared with print news sources. But credibility can be an issue, and a reader must be careful to discern what is journalism and what is, for example, a blog post.

OPINION JOURNALISM

How wonderful to be paid to express what you think! That's the job of opinion journalists, who cover a subject from their own thoughts and viewpoints rather than entirely on objective facts. When a piece of journalism is an opinion piece, rather than an unbiased one, it must be clear to the reader that what is being expressed is in fact the viewpoint of the writer—perhaps you agree with them or perhaps they make your blood boil. Either way, it's legitimate as long as it's clearly opinion. This type of journalism can be found in print, online, and broadcast outlets.

SPORTS JOURNALISM

For sports fans out there, this may be the dream job for you. A sports journalist focuses on the subject of athletic news—team rankings and standings, investigative stories of financial or drug scandals, coverage of major sporting events, and profiles of star athletes. Sports journalists can be opinion or investigative journalists, depending on the type of stories they cover. This type of journalism can be found in both print and broadcast media. Sports commentating is a form of sports journalism in broadcast and online journalism.

TRADE JOURNALISM

With a focus on a particular industry—oil, health care, financial—trade journalists cover news related to specific business sectors or a particular industry or field. Trade journalists detail movements and developments in business that impact people involved in that field. Trade journalism can take the form of different genres and is common in print, digital, and broadcast media.

ENTERTAINMENT JOURNALISM

For those who like to live glamorously, entertainment journalism focuses on pop culture figures and trends, as well as business news related to the entertainment industry. Profiles of celebrities and their work and lives and live coverage of big events like film premieres and award ceremonies fall under entertainment news. Entertainment journalism can take the form of different genres and is common in print, digital, and broadcast media.

POLITICAL JOURNALISM

An important role in the world of media and journalism is political journalism, which is the type that focuses on government, politics, and potential political candidates. This can include local news (relating to anything from school board elections to the decision of a mayor), national news (e.g., a speech by the president or a vote in the Supreme Court), or international news (coverage of war zones, international environmental, or financial laws, etc.). It is so important because politics touches on every part of everyone's life, from their freedoms to their finances. Journalists and media professionals with this as their emphasis wear various hats, such as that of watchdog, investigative, and opinion journalist. Political journalism applies to print, digital, and broadcast media.

BROADCAST JOURNALISM

This is a form of journalism everyone will be familiar with. While it can include various types of journalism as previously defined and cover many of the same topics (such as local, national, or global news, entertainment, sports, or weather), the format in which it is delivered differs from print or online.

Broadcast journalism is any journalism that reports its news to the public through media such as radio and television. It can be produced in various formats: via a newscaster reading from a written script, a live interview with a newsworthy guest, or a recorded report from a location where the news is happening, such as during an important speech given by a politician.

Although the terms *journalist* and *media* may at first conjure images of a reporting busily typing away trying to make deadline, professionals in these fields work in an endless variety of locations using a range of technologies, methods, and tools to deliver their stories.
CYANO66/ISTOCK/GETTY IMAGES.

Although certainly there are other forms of media and journalism, including book publishing and documentary filmmaking, which also rely on the same skills and approaches as, say, magazine publishing and a nightly newscast, this book will focus on careers with newspapers (online and in print), magazines, television, radio, and online broadcasting channels for news.

CULTIVATING A VOICE AND AN AUDIENCE AS A BLOGGER

Sheila Quirke
COURTESY OF SHEILA QUIRKE.

Sheila Quirke is a freelance writer and blogger (Mary Tyler Mom) living in Chicago with her husband and two sons. Trained and experienced as a clinical social worker, she shifted gears after the death of her daughter from cancer. Sheila's words have appeared at *ChicagoNow*, *Huffington Post*, *Chicago Tribune*, *Scary Mommy*, *mom.me*, and in the anthology *Listen to Your Mother: What She Said Then, What We're Saying Now*, published in 2015. Her blog, *Mary Tyler Mom Writes*, focuses on themes of grief, parenting, social justice issues, gun violence, public education, politics and, sometimes, just to keep it light, fashion and TV shows

Why did you choose to become a blogger?

I started writing an online journal with my husband just a few days after our daughter was diagnosed with an aggressive brain tumor. Initially, it was meant to be an efficient communication tool for friends and family, updating them on our girl without needing to repeat information. She was in treatment for over two years, and we sustained that journal throughout her illness. The writing was both a release and a tool. I valued the connection it provided and being able to express myself through language during a devastating experience. Giving voice to my worst fears was cathartic and helped me put those fears someplace so I could bet there for my dear girl. After our daughter died, my husband stopped writing, but I continued. It turns out, having the back-and-forth with readers was healing and productive for my grief.

After our daughter's death, I made a conscious decision to create a blog. This was in 2011 when blogging was in its heyday. I was returning to my career in social work but didn't want to lose the connection writing had provided me. I also didn't want to keep focusing on grief, so the original intent of *Mary Tyler Mom*, my blogging persona, was to cover topics relevant to being a working parent. That lasted all of six months before I "outed" myself as a grieving mother and began to write about child loss as a major focus on the blog. Speaking from that place of authenticity is when I found my audience, and *Mary Tyler Mom* really took off.

What is a typical writing day for you?

Before these current challenging days during a global pandemic, the best time to write was after I had gotten my kids off to school in the morning. Arrive home, tidy a bit or plan household errands, start thinking while doing the repetitive tasks of running a home with young children, sit down at the computer, and write. Ideas are kept on the notepad of my phone, so they aren't lost in the minute. I also enjoy opining on current issues or news of the day, so writing often involves research. It's not unusual for me to race the clock to publish something and cross post on my social media channels just as I am dashing off for school dismissal. Once the kids are back home, writing gets a lot more complicated, so if I miss those morning kid-free hours, the task and demands of writing become both more complicated and less likely to be achieved.

What's the best part of your job?

I love the independence of writing—just me and the keyboard, typing away. I love creating an online community around my words. I love the challenge of capturing the nuance of something ephemeral or complicated, whether it is a thorny political issue or working to explain the pain of packing up a closet full of little girl clothes that will never be worn again because that little girl has died. When I am successful, I feel accomplished, productive, relevant, connected. The connection with readers is probably the best part of blogging. It is still surprising and humbling that strangers on the Internet take the time to read what I write and seem to care about what I have to say.

What's the worst or most challenging part of being a blogger?

As my platform expanded and my blog became more well-known, I was honored to get shots at different types of writing opportunities. It is wonderfully flattering to be recognized for my writing when writing is something that I still feel "happened" to me. It never feels like something I set out to do, but instead, something I fell into that somehow clicked. "Imposter syndrome" is a very real thing for me. Things that contribute to that are how I came to writing, that I originally gained prominence as a "mommy blogger," and that I did not become a successful blogger until well into my forties. That sense of feeling unworthy or not qualified can hinder the hustle needed to remain successful in this arena and branch out into other forms of writing like paid freelance work or content marketing.

What's the most surprising thing about being a blogger/writer?

By nature, I am shy and a wee bit insecure, though I have always had strong opinions on things and have enjoyed a good debate. Cultivating my blog has provided me a platform that has enabled me to strengthen my voice and my passionate opinions without challenging my innate shyness and insecurities. I can roar like a lion, and do, from the comfort of my dining room table. Then, inevitably, when a strong opinion about a controversial subject is expressed, someone will object. It is the nature of the beast, and honestly the mark of a successful blog. If you're doing it right, your words will provoke, but dealing with the fallout of angry readers sometimes feels above my pay grade.

Additionally, there is the potency of being thought of as an "influencer" by folks who don't know you, then turning off the computer and having a six-year-old refuse to brush his teeth or pick up his dirty socks. Kiddo! Don't you know I'm kind of a big deal on the Internet?! Children will always keep you humble.

What kinds of qualities do you think one needs to be successful at this role?

H-U-S-T-L-E is the name of the game in blogging. One of my early champions was a fellow blogger who had amassed a Facebook community around her blog of over a million followers. She and I became friendly when I was just starting out, and she gave me sound advice that has never failed me, "Do the work." The work of blogging is to keep producing—keep writing, keep engaging your audience, keep flexing and growing, keep feeding that Internet content beast.

The social media landscape has changed dramatically in the past five years, with an emphasis on video (YouTube and TikTok), imagery (Instagram), and hot take sound bites (Twitter). In some ways, blogging and all those words feel like they are from the Stone Age. But still, there is a place for words that don't involve video and require more than 280 characters (Medium is rocking). The relationship that a blogger builds with their reader is an effective tool. It is authentic, relatable, consistent, and trusted. Honor that, do the work, and success will follow.

How do you combat burnout?

I wish I knew! These past few years have kicked my blogging patootie! The world is a noisy place right now, made more so by social media and unprecedented geopolitical unrest. Adding to the drowning din often feels counterproductive and not particularly useful. I got quiet for a couple of years recently—I stopped "doing the work" required of blogging, and my stats reflect that. Burnout is part of the issue, but self-preservation is part of it, too. Sending controversial opinions out into the universe at this particular moment is taking a different kind of a toll that feels heavier than it used to feel.

One thing that has helped me is shifting gears. After getting quiet for a few years, I have gotten more selective and nuanced about what thoughts inside my head are deserving of my platform. I am more judicious; I read and listen more. That has helped. I have also focused on cultivating more paid writing opportunities based on melding my areas of expertise—combining my social work background, personal and professional experiences in the medical field, and writing. That is a valuable niche, it turns out, so I have enjoyed and benefited from putting the focus less on my personal opinions, and more on something external to me. Finding clients who value what I can uniquely provide has helped me start doing the work of blogging once again, just in a different context.

What would you tell a young person who is thinking about becoming a blogger?
Do it! Find your passion and stay authentic. It sounds clichéd, but it isn't. Learning how to craft your thoughts into your voice using words will benefit you no matter what direction your life takes you. Embrace that blogging is an endeavor that is equal parts building community and self-disclosure. When you find the right balance between those two things, it is a powerful and valuable tool.

The media and journalism industry has changed and evolved over time, responding to such factors as demand for up-to-date news and twenty-four-hour cable networks as well as technological advancements, including the Internet.
SUKSAN YODYIAM/ISTOCK/GETTY IMAGES.

FIVE HISTORIC EXAMPLES OF INVESTIGATIVE JOURNALISM MAKING A DIFFERENCE

A career within journalism and the media can be challenging and educational and broaden your worldview, but it is also a field that can enable you to have a real impact on the world, how powers are used and abused, the issues we are confronted by, and the people who are otherwise overlooked who deserve recognition.

In several instances across history, journalists have worked tirelessly to follow leads, do their research, and keep pursuing the truth regardless of hurdles, fatigue, or discouragement. Here, we outline five key moments where journalists made a lasting difference, as identified by Brookings.edu.[2]

Ida Tarbell Takes on the Standard Oil Company

Late in the nineteenth century and early in twentieth, there was a big public surge to do away with corruption or unfair practices in government and big business. The latter mostly focused on monopolistic practices, in which one leader of an industry got too big, thereby reducing the space for competition and having too much control for the public good. Writing for *McClure's Magazine*, in 1902 and 1903 journalist Ida Tarbell, who had shifted careers from schoolteacher to change-making journalist, produced several articles chronicling the activities of the Standard Oil Company, which was owned by John D. Rockefeller. Because of the awareness her articles brought to the issue of monopolization of the oil business, the US Supreme Court found the company to be in violation of the Sherman Antitrust Act in 1911, causing its breakup.

Exposing the Unsanitary Practices of Chicago's Meatpacking Industry

Although this mention focuses on what in the end was a work of fiction, it has its roots entirely in investigative journalism. Perhaps you have read the 1906 novel *The Jungle*. Written by Upton Sinclair, the book sheds a disturbing and stomach-churning light on the meatpacking industry in 1900 in the city of the Chicago, where the meat industry was big business—and was the center of meat processing for the entire country. Sinclair went undercover to work at a meatpacking plant and later exposed the unsanitary practices in the plant and the appalling conditions under which the immigrant laborers employed there were forced to work. The year his book was published was also the year the Pure Food and Drug Act of 1906 and the Federal Meat

Inspection Act of 1906 were passed in the United States, so Sinclair had definitely hit on an important issue impacting the health of millions.

A Reporter Rattles the US President for Doing His Job Too Well in Wartime

Although it's expected to some degree for someone in public office—particularly the president of the United States—to be at occasional odds with the press, whose job it is to play watchdog to politicians, among other entities of power, in October 1963 President John F. Kennedy took the (at the time) unusual step of going so far as to ask a national newspaper to cease one of its reporters from covering a story. Journalist David Halberstam, reporting from Saigon, Vietnam, for the *New York Times*, was apparently doing too fine a job covering the war the United States was engaged in there. Although the US government attempted to portray the decisions, behaviors, and results of their wartime policies positively, Halberstam was uncovering a less-optimistic story. President Kennedy requested the reporter be removed from Vietnam to keep him silent. Halberstam, on the other hand, held the view that a journalist had to report the news, whether it was good for America or not. He won a Pulitzer Prize for his work in 1964.

Exposing the Watergate Scandal

This may be the most well-known story of journalism triumphing over corrupt politicians in (relatively) recent times. What began as a break-in at the offices of the Democratic National Committee at the Watergate Complex in Washington, DC, in June 1972 (an election year), unraveled into a massive scandal that led to the eventual resignation of then-president Richard Nixon. Two reporters working for *the Washington Post*, Bob Woodward and Carl Bernstein, picked up on a key detail that one of the burglars arrested was actually on the president's payroll. Following this lead, they exposed that the White House had orchestrated the break-in to gain advantage in the upcoming presidential election. The paper won a Pulitzer Prize in 1973 for its coverage of this story.

Exposing Unethical Surveillance Activities of the National Security Agency

At the start of 2013, two newspapers—the *Washington Post* and the *Guardian* (UK)—broke a big story at roughly the same time. The focus of the news was the US National Security Agency (NSA) and its practices of using its power through various programs that abused the privacy rights of citizens. The whistleblower—an employee of a private consulting firm at the time, later revealed to be Edward Snowden—contacted the press and leaked confidential documents to them to substantiate his assertions. A series of articles was published by both the *Washington Post* and *The Guardian* exposing the NSA and earning them a shared Pulitzer Prize for their work.

The Pulitzer Prize is an important, coveted award that annually acknowledges achievement in newspaper, broadcast, and online journalism in the United States, as well as in literature and musical composition. It is named after its founder, journalist Joseph Pulitzer, who established the award in 1917. The prize, administered by Columbia University in New York, is awarded in twenty-one separate categories, and recipients receive a cash award of fifteen thousand dollars.

Careers within the Fields of Media and Journalism

Although this book will cover as many of these careers as possible, it will focus mostly on the following:

- *Editors in chief:* Editors in chief have a high-level, important function at publications including newspapers and magazines as well as broadcast media. They are charged with overseeing the work of all staff editors and have authority over what is published or included in a broadcast.
- *Editors:* Editors or senior editors are responsible for a particular section of a publication (such as a features editor at a newspaper) or segment of a broadcast. They make decisions about what stories are included and oversee staff.
- *Copyeditors:* Copyeditors have the important task of making sure all work is grammatically correct and spelled correctly, that proper punctuation is used, and that the text adheres to the conventions outlined in the style guide. In some instances, copyeditors also are responsible for writing headlines.
- *Proofreaders:* Proofreaders also check a text for spelling, punctuation, and grammar and, in the print world, usually do this after the publication has been laid out (so that it looks as it will appear in print). This means

a proofreader is also charged with resolving any layout issues, such as an article running too long to fit in the space allotted on the page.

- *Reporters*: Reporters are journalism/media professionals whose job it is to uncover, follow, research, and report on the news, either online, in print, or via broadcast channels.

- *Correspondents*: Correspondents are journalists who work from a particular location, delivering on-the-scene reports for print or online news outlets, television, or radio. Sometimes correspondents are sent to faraway locations, including other countries or remote areas of the world.

- *Broadcast journalists*: Broadcast journalists work in the television, radio, or Internet broadcasting arena and not in print or online magazine or newspapers.

- *Photojournalists*: Photojournalists tell a story with an image. Sometimes photojournalists work alongside reporters, and other times the image itself tells the story with no accompanying text.

Although we are not covering this in-depth in this book, editorial cartoonists or political cartoonists, also play an important role in media and journalism. Such cartoons that appear in newspapers and news magazines express opinions or viewpoints about current events through drawing and occasionally captions. As with any content, the cartoons also go through an editorial review process with a publication.

The Pros and Cons of the Media and Journalism Field

As with any career, one in journalism and media has upsides and downsides. But also true is that one person's "pro" is another person's "con." If you love working in teams and collaborating with others, then this could well be the right job for you. But if you prefer to work solo, it's probably going to be frustrating for you at times. Equally if you like the rush of a hurried deadline, ever-changing specifications and due dates, and don't mind working long hours at times and weekends, then you will get a charge out of a career in journalism and media. But if you prefer a 9-to-5 life and a predictable schedule and don't want to bring work home with you, again, that could be a serious red flag.

Although it's one thing to read about the pros and cons of a particular career, the best way to really get a feel for what a typical day is like on the job and what the challenges and rewards are is to talk to someone who is already working in the profession or who has in the past.

Although each profession within the media and journalism field is different, there are some generalizations that can be made when it comes to what is most challenging about the field and most gratifying.

Here are some general pros:

- You get to do what you love and apply your research, reporting, interviewing, and writing or broadcasting skills to a satisfying career.
- The work is incredibly creative and challenging and never routine. Almost every day, every story, every issue, or broadcast—whatever your experience—will be different from the next.
- In this competitive field, you will have colleagues who share your passion and from whom you can learn.
- It is a constantly evolving field with new trends and innovations and an endless opportunity for learning.
- There's a vast degree of variety in work environments, from large corporations to start-ups to freelance work from anywhere.
- It's a field in which you can make a real difference by shedding light on issues, people, and events that you are passionate about.

And here are some general cons:

- The working hours can be long and irregular. You can expect at times to work early and late hours and also on weekends to meet a pressing deadline or react to any unpredictable issues or situations that may arise.
- As far as salaries and growth in media and journalism, the predictions show a decline.
- It is high-pressure field that requires an ability to manage stress well as well as to multitask.
- It is an extremely competitive field, and breaking in and then advancing to the next level can take a lot of time, hard work, and patience.

> "I have worked with people who have been trained up right from school to college or university and worked with someone who joined our team after working as a tram driver. The one thing that has connected them all is a willingness to learn and adapt."—Fiona Kelly, senior editor, television news

How Healthy Is the Job Market?

To be completely frank, the data regarding career outlook (which refers to growth in both opportunity and salary indication) for media and journalism jobs is not fantastically optimistic, showing an actual decline in the decade between 2018 and 2028. As mentioned previously, according to the US Bureau of Labor Statistics (BLS),[3] jobs for reporters and correspondents will decline by 12 percent from 2018 to 2028, and during the same period, jobs for editors will decrease by 3 percent and jobs for photographers will decrease by 6 percent.

But this is at odds with the level of interest people are showing in entering the field. Universities offering programs in journalism and media studies (we will look at this closely in chapter 3) report a notable increase in applicants,[4] up to 24 percent in some cases, which shows that young people are interested in keeping the field alive and thriving.

WHAT IS A MEDIAN INCOME?

Throughout your job search, you might hear the term *median income*. What does it mean? Some people believe it's the same thing as *average income*, but that's not correct. Although the median income and average income might sometimes be similar, they are calculated in different ways.

The true definition of median income is the income at which half of the workers earn more than that income and the other half of workers earn less. If this is complicated, think of it this way: Suppose there are five employees in a company, each with varying skills and experience. Here are their salaries:

- $42,500
- $48,250
- $51,600

- $63,120
- $86,325

What is the median income? In this case, the median income is $51,600, because of the five total positions listed, it is in the middle. Two salaries are higher than $51,600, and two are lower.

The average income is simply the total of all salaries, divided by the number of total jobs. In this case, the average income is $58,359.

Why does this matter? The median income is a more accurate way to measure the various incomes in a set because it's less likely to be influenced by extremely high or low numbers in the total group of salaries. For example, in our example of five incomes, the highest income ($86,325) is much higher than the other incomes, and therefore, it makes the average income ($58,359) well higher than most incomes in the group. So if you base your income expectations on the average, you'll likely be disappointed to eventually learn that most incomes are below it.

But if you look at median income, you'll always know that half the people are above it, and half are below it. That way, depending on your level of experience and training, you'll have a better estimate of where you'll end up on the salary spectrum.

It's difficult to predict what will happen in the future with a career field as broad, as necessary, as in-demand, and as ever-changing as journalism and media. Business practices like forming monopolies of media corporations and shutting down newspapers because of loss of revenue are obstacles the industry is facing, and these are no doubt issues that will need to be addressed. For now, let's look at the outlook for various jobs with journalism and media.

The Bureau of Labor Statistics and other sites offering information on annual and hourly salaries for particular professions do not distinguish among editor, copyeditor, and proofreader or between correspondent and reporter—broadcast or print.

EDITOR IN CHIEF[5]

- Hourly pay: Not listed
- Annual wage: $76,258
- Projected growth (2018–2028): –8% decline

EDITOR[6]

- Hourly pay: $29.50 per hour
- Annual pay: $61,370 per year
- Projected growth (2018–2028): –8% decline

COPYEDITOR[7]

- Hourly pay: $29.50 per hour
- Annual pay: $61,370 per year
- Projected growth (2018–2028): –8% decline

PROOFREADER[8]

- Hourly pay: $29.50 per hour
- Annual pay: $61,370 per year
- Projected growth (2018–2028): –8% decline

REPORTER[9]

- Hourly pay: $20.91 per hour
- Annual pay: $43,490 per year
- Projected growth (2018–2028): –10% decline

CORRESPONDENT[10]

- Hourly pay: $20.91 per hour
- Annual pay: $43,490 per year
- Projected growth (2018–2028): –10% decline

BROADCAST JOURNALIST[11]

- Hourly pay: $20.91 per hour
- Annual pay: $43,490 per year
- Projected growth (2018–2028): –10% decline

PHOTOGRAPHERS[12]

- Hourly pay: $17.44 per hour
- Annual pay: $36,280 per year
- Projected growth (2018–2028): –6% decline

Many journalists do work full-time for a particular company, radio station, television network, or publication. As of 2008, actually, the BLS reported that 37,995[13] reporters and correspondents were employed full-time, but the number of people registered as self-employed writers and authors—which also includes freelancers who work for news organizations and blogs—was 83,968.[14] Later in the book, we will explore more about freelancing as a career option for journalists and media professionals.

Am I Right for a Media and Journalism Career?

This is a tough question to answer because really the answer can only come from you. But don't despair: There are plenty of resources both online and elsewhere that can help you find the answer by guiding you through the types of questions and considerations that will bring you to your conclusion. These are covered in more detail in the next chapter. But for now, let's look at the general demands and responsibilities of a media and journalism career—as were mentioned previously in the section on pros and cons—and suggest some questions that may help you discover whether such a profession is a good match for your personality, interests, and the general lifestyle you want to have in the future.

Of course no job is going to match your personality or fit your every desire, especially when you are just starting out. There are, however, some aspects to a job that may be so unappealing or simply mismatched that you may decide to opt for something else, or equally you may be so drawn to a feature of a job that any downsides are not that important.

Obviously having an ability and a passion for news, for analyzing facts and events, for writing and storytelling, and for continuously learning is key to success in this field, but there are other factors to keep in mind. One way to see if you may be cut out for a career in media and journalism is to ask yourself the following questions:

- **Would I prefer to be active and moving around during work, or would I rather mostly stay put behind a desk?**
  The good news is that with a media and journalism career, it's possible to have one or the other or even both. If you are a correspondent, for example, you may have the opportunity to travel as far away and re-motely as you wish; if you choose a career as a desk editor for a daily newspaper, then—as you might guess—you will be working from an office.
- **When something goes wrong, can I think quickly on my feet to find a solution? Do I have the leadership skills to direct others to help solve problems?**
  The news is ever-changing. New facts come in, circumstances shift, the unexpected occurs at any time in your production or publishing process, and journalists and media professionals have to be quick on their feet to respond and adjust to unpredictability.
- **Am I a highly creative, analytical thinker who comes up with lots of ideas? Am I equally able to let an idea go or adjust it?**
  Journalism and media jobs attract creative people, but in most cases (certainly if you are working for an editor in chief) you will not have full

creative authority over what you want to write or produce. Teamwork and cooperation are key in this profession.

- **Am I genuinely interested in other people, other points of view, and seeking the truth no matter what?**
  Journalists have a responsibility to be unbiased and to be ethical in their practices, such as only using valid sources to support stories and not using their role to misrepresent a situation. It's necessary to be passionate about the news but equally so to be able to be objective.

- **Can I consistently deal with people in a professional, friendly way?**
  Communication—naturally—is key to success in the journalism and media field. Writing and speaking in a highly tuned, effective, coherent, and engaging manner is a massive part of the job, but equally interpersonal communication with the team, with people covered in stories, with the people interviewed and interacted with to research a story is enormously important.

- **Do I have an overly excited attention to detail and an inability to leave any stone unturned?**
  Details are the key to authenticity in research and reporting, as well as in producing high-quality news items worth publishing in print, broadcasting, or posting online. You must be someone who doesn't leave a question unanswered. You must have perfectionist tendencies and be thorough.

- **At the same time, can I work to deadline and function under pressure?**
  Here's the trickiest part: A journalist or media professional must operate in the real world of deadlines. This is a career choice with a high level of stress and pressure, and to be successful you must be able to thrive in whatever deadline stress you find yourself in.

A SNAPSHOT OF THE LIFE OF A PHOTOJOURNALIST

Robin Barret
COURTESY OF ROBIN BARRET.

Robin Barrett has been a professional photographer for more than twenty years working as a staff photographer at the *San Francisco Chronicle* and freelancing for major news agencies like the Associated Press and other worldwide news organizations. Barrett has worked in New York City, Washington, DC, San Diego, and San Francisco and traveled to every state except Alaska covering a wide variety of photo assignments. Robin has a BA in journalism and photography.

Why did you choose to become a photographer?

My dad and grandfather were always into photography, and I developed an interest at a young age. In high school, I took my first photography darkroom class, and having teachers believe in my artistic talent propelled me to continue pursuing photography in college. As an event photographer and newspaper staff photographer in college, it gave me a front-row seat to all college sporting events, big-ticket events, and behind-the-scenes activities. Photojournalism was thrilling and fun, so I decided that's what I would do as a profession.

What is a typical day on the job for you?

That's the beauty of being a photographer. There is no typical day on the job. My day could have begun photographing horseback riding lessons in a barn to photographing the president of the United States at a fundraising event during an election year. I've ridden on competition sailboats, hung out the side of a helicopter, sped around a racetrack in a pace car, and climbed one hundred feet into a redwood tree.

What's the best part of your job?

I have photographed A-list celebrities and professional sports and news events that have changed the lives of so many. Creating those photographs was exciting but also devastating and I believe they are important historical records. One of my favorite parts of my job as a photographer has been making photos that have personal meaning for people. I once photographed a father and son at elementary- school bingo night, and the photo was published in our local paper. The next week I got a call from the mom and she wanted to tell me how much that photo meant to her son. She told me that her son had a terminal illness, and when he saw his photo with his dad in the paper it delighted him. She said he had the biggest smile and slept with and carried that photo everywhere. I captured that photo twenty-six years ago.

What's the worst or most challenging part of your job?
Photographing scenes where people have died has been the worst and most challenging part of my job. Unfortunately, there are murders, car accidents, terrorism, and ruthlessness in this world, and photojournalists have to capture those scenes.

What's the most surprising thing about your job?
Every photo assignment is always different, and there are always surprises. When I was still shooting with film, I was photographing the Chicago Cubs' Sammy Sosa at bat during a game against the San Francisco Giants, and his bat broke. I didn't find out until hours later that I had captured a rare photo of him swinging, the ball in frame and the bat split in three pieces, also in the frame. That photo was published over two pages in *ESPN* magazine, and I got paid about $400. That was a wonderful surprise and the best sports photo I ever captured.

What kinds of qualities do you think one needs to be successful at this job?
Photographers should be curious, patient, calm, and analytical. Photographers need to be observant and analyze a scene to determine the best way to capture a person or an event to clearly tell the story to viewers without words.

How do you combat burnout?
Burnout is a common problem in the photojournalism field. Photo assignments can take hours and sometimes days depending on what it is. This can affect personal relationships. The other issue is the subject matter of some assignments like death and dying that can be incredibly difficult to process once the assignments are complete. When I wasn't taking pictures, I was doing something athletic with friends, like training for marathons, playing softball, riding bicycles, hiking, and lots of other fun activities. Having a balance is very important.

What would you tell a young person who is thinking about becoming a photographer?
Photojournalism and event photography are very different nowadays then when I became a professional. When I entered the profession, everything was captured on film (digital didn't exist yet), and only professionals and serious hobbyists purchased the big expensive cameras. Nowadays everyone has a smartphone, and professionals compete with everyone else to carve out a field in photography. Photography staff jobs are not as common, but they do exist. To be competitive,

you need to be a technical expert, a software expert in not just Photoshop but other relevant editing programs. You may need to be able to not only capture still photographs but also video and edit both separately or creatively combine the two. Look for photography jobs with the federal government, private companies, or public relations firms. Freelance photographers nowadays need to develop relationships with companies and be what is now called an influencer photographer. There will always be a demand for professional photographers, whether at weddings, capturing families, events, or products.

Summary

This chapter covered a lot of ground as far as looking more closely at the various types of professions and jobs that exist within the overarching field of media and journalism. The news and information business is one that entails many different forms of story investigating and delivering, from deeply researched exposés that probe a topic for an extended period of time to opinion pieces in which the writer's viewpoint is expressed. These stories can be shared digitally or in print, as well as broadcast such as via radio or television.

The future and growth of media and journalism is difficult to define in certain terms because recent years have seen job losses and changes in financial profit models (in cases where advertising for print publications as a source of revenue has been in decline), there has been a surge of interest in studying media and journalism, and people are hungrier than ever to get reliable, honest, and timely news. So although there have been some highs and lows and shifts in how the business of media is managed, the need for and desire for news and people who can deliver it will not diminish.

Here are some ideas to take away with you as you move on to the next chapter:

- The field of media and journalism is a broad one that is ever-changing. It carries with it a responsibility to deliver news that is carefully supported and researched.

- In many media and journalism jobs, no day is exactly like the next. Professionals in these areas often work long hours on shifting stories with tight deadlines. It can involve global travel, or you can expect to sit behind a desk editing and publishing the news.
- As a journalist or media professional, you can choose from many different types of stories you want to cover, from entertainment to international politics to the tuna fish industry. Everywhere you look, there's news to be covered.
- Given all you now know about media and journalism, you may still be questioning whether such a career is right for you. This chapter provided some questions that can help you visualize yourself in real-world situations you can expect to face on the job, such as whether you see yourself collaborating in teams and working toward frequently moving targets such as schedules.

Assuming you are now more enthusiastic than ever about pursuing a career in journalism and the media, in the next chapter we will look more closely at how you can refine your choice to a more specific job. It offers tips and advice and how to find the role and work environment that will be most satisfying to you and what steps you can start taking—immediately!—toward reaching your future career goals.

2

Forming a Career Plan

No pressure, but choosing a career is one of the most important decisions you will make in your life. There are so many options available, and it is easy to feel overwhelmed. Particularly if you have many passions and interests, it can be hard to narrow your options down. That you are reading this book means you have decided to investigate a career in the media and journalism industry, which means you have already discovered a passion for creativity, gathering knowledge, interacting with people, sharing and hearing stories, and continuous learning.

But even within the media and journalism industry, there are many choices, including what role you want to pursue, what work environment you desire, and what type of work schedule best fits your lifestyle. It's a lot to think about, but fortunately it's also exciting to consider your options, particularly because it's a decision that is primarily based on aspects of you (your interests, natural gifts, curiosities) that you know more about than anyone else.

This may all sound dramatic and even scary. Keep in mind as you consider your career options that it is common to change your mind or shift gears at any stage in your career. Be thoughtful about your decisions, but don't put too much pressure on yourself. It's not a case of only getting one chance to decide.

A career in journalism and the media offers a lot of choice and variety. Before you can plan the path to a successful career in the industry—such as by committing to a college program—it's helpful to develop an understanding of what role you want to have and in what environment you wish to work. Do you want to work in an established, multinational media company, or do you prefer the more entrepreneurial feel of a start-up? Are you attracted to the life of a freelancer, or do you long to travel to faraway and even dangerous places? Or maybe you want to start your own online magazine. Are you willing to relocate? Travel a lot? These are all things to consider.

It's also important to think about how much education you would like to pursue. Depending on your ultimate career goal, the steps to getting there differ. Jobs in journalism will typically require a bachelor's degree or higher. You can choose to study anything that relates to journalism, communications, writing, or a subject that you want your journalism to focus on, such as finance or law; the choices are many, and we will look at them a bit in this chapter and even more specifically, as well as discussing particular schools that offer programs of interest.

Deciding on a career means asking yourself big questions, but there are several tools and assessment tests that can help you determine what your personal strengths and aptitudes are and with which career fields and environments they best align. These tools guide you to think about important factors in choosing a career path, such as how you respond to pressure and how effectively you work an communicate with people, and how much you enjoy doing so.

YOUR PASSIONS, ABILITIES, AND INTERESTS: IN JOB FORM!

Think about how you've done at school and how things have worked out at any temporary or part-time jobs you've had so far. What are you really good at, in your opinion? And what have other people told you you're good at? What are you not good at right now, but you would like to become better at? What are you not good at, and you're okay with not getting better at?

Now forget about work for a minute. In fact, forget about needing to ever have a job again. You won the lottery—congratulations! Now answer these questions: What are your favorite three ways of spending your time? For each one of those things, can you describe why you think you are attracted to it? If you could get up tomorrow and do anything you wanted all day long, what would it be? These questions can be fun but can also lead you to your true passions. The next step is to find the job that sparks your passions.

This chapter explores the educational requirements for various careers within the media industry, as well as options for where to go for help when planning your path to the career you want. It offers advice on how to begin preparing for your career path at any age or stage in your education, including in high school.

Planning the Plan

So where to begin? Before taking the leap and applying to or committing in your mind to a particular college, there are other considerations and steps you can take to map out your plan for pursuing your career. Preparing your career plan begins with developing a clear understanding of what your actual career goal is.

Planning your career path means asking yourself questions that will help shape a clearer picture of what your long-term career goals are and what steps to take to achieve them. When considering these questions, it's important to prioritize your answers—when listing your skills, for example, put them in order of strongest to weakest. When considering questions relating to how you want to balance your career with the rest of your nonwork life, such as family and hobbies, really think about what your top priorities are and in what order.

The following questions are helpful to think about when planning your career path.

- Think about your interests outside the work context. How do you like to spend your free time? What inspires you? What kind of people do you like to surround yourself with, and how do you best learn? What do you really love doing? (Hint: If you find you dislike reading or following the news, journalism may not be for you.)
- Brainstorm a list of the various career choices within the media industry that you are interested in pursuing (think about being an editor of a monthly fashion magazine versus the lead anchor of an international news channel). Organize the list in order of which careers you find most appealing and then list what it is about each that attracts you. This can be anything from work environment to geographical location to the degree to which you would work with other people in a particular role.
- Research information on each job on your career choices list. You can find job descriptions, salary indications, career outlook, salary, and

educational requirements online, for example. Some of this information was provided in chapter 1 of this book.

- Consider your personality traits. This is important to finding which jobs "fit" you and which almost certainly do not. How do you respond to stress and pressure? Do you consider yourself a strong communicator? Do you work well in teams or prefer to work independently? Do you consider yourself creative? How do you respond to criticism? Are you curious and thorough? All of these are important to keep in mind to ensure you choose a career path that makes you happy and in which you can thrive.

- Although a career choice is obviously a huge factor in your future, it's important to consider what other factors feature in your vision of your ideal life. Think about how your career will fit in with the rest of your life, including whether you want to live in a big city or small town, how much flexibility you want in your schedule, how much autonomy you want in your work, and what your ultimate career goal is.

- The media and journalism industry is a competitive one that, particularly when you are starting out in your career, will require you to work hard (sometimes only for experience, as with an internship), work long hours, take the less glamorous assignments or tasks, and not earn a particularly impressive salary. Applications to journalism schools are growing in number, even as career outlook data looks discouraging (see chapter 1 for more on that), so competition is on the rise. Because succeeding in the journalism and media field requires so much commitment, it's important to think about how willing you are to put in long hours and perform what can be demanding work—without burning out.

- Although there are many lucrative careers in the journalism and media field, many job opportunities that offer experience to newcomers and recent graduates can come with relatively low salaries. What are your pay expectations, now and in the future?

Posing these questions to yourself, thinking about them deeply, and answering them honestly will help make your career goals clearer and guide you in knowing which steps you will need to take to get there.

Making decisions about your career path should not cause you stress or anxiety, but it is an important task. Take your time and think thoughtfully—and take notes!—about what type of job, function, and working environment and schedule might best fit your personality.
FIZKES/ISTOCK/GETTY IMAGES.

Where to Go for Help

Again, the process of deciding on and planning a career path is daunting. In many ways, the range of choices of careers available today is a wonderful thing. It allows us to refine our career goals and customize them to our own lives and personalities. In other ways, though, too much choice can be extremely daunting and require a lot of soul-searching to navigate clearly.

Answering questions about your habits, characteristics, interests, and personality can be challenging. Identifying and prioritizing all of your ambitions, interests, and passions can be overwhelming and complicated. It's not always easy to see ourselves objectively or see a way to achieve what matters most to us. But there are several resources and approaches to help guide you in drawing conclusions about these important questions.

- Take a career assessment test to help you answer questions about what career best suits you. There are several available online.
- Consult with a career or personal coach to help you refine your understanding of your goals and how to pursue them.
- Talk with professionals working in the job you are considering and ask them what they enjoy about their work, what they find the most challenging, and what path they followed to get there.
- Educate yourself as much as possible about the industry: which technologies are changing how people report, deliver, and receive the news, for example. Stay abreast of the industry, no matter which role you wish to pursue.
- If possible, arrange to shadow someone working in the field you are considering. This will enable you to experience in person what the atmosphere is like, what a typical workday entails, how coworkers interact with each other and with management, and how well you can see yourself thriving in that role and work culture.
- Work on your portfolio. Don't wait until you can be paid professionally to start building a body of work, be it published or not. Start a blog (but keep it professional) or write letters to the editor in your local paper . . . whatever shows your writing prowess and interest in current events.

ONLINE RESOURCES TO HELP YOU PLAN YOUR PATH

The Internet is an excellent source of advice and assessment tools that can help you find and figure out how to pursue your career path. Some of these tools focus on your personality and aptitude, and others can help you identify and improve your skills to prepare for your career.

In addition to the sites listed here, you can use the Internet to find a career coach or life coach near you; many offer their services online as well. Job sites such as LinkedIn are a good place to search for people working in a profession you'd like to learn more about or to explore the types of jobs available in the media and journalism industry.

- At educations.com, you will find a career test designed to help you find the job of your dreams. Visit https://www.educations.com/career-test to take the test.
- The *Princeton Review* has created a career quiz that focuses on personal interests. Visit https://www.princetonreview.com/quiz/career-quiz.
- The Bureau of Labor Statistics provides information, including quizzes and videos, to help students up to twelfth grade explore various career paths. The site also provides general information on career prospects and salaries. Visit www.BLS.gov to find these resources.

Young adults with disabilities can face additional challenges when planning a career path. Disabilities, Opportunities, Internetworking, and Technology (DO-IT) is an organization dedicated to promoting career and education inclusion for everyone. Its website[1] contains a wealth of information and tools to help all young people plan a career path, including self-assessment tests and career exploration questionnaires.

Making High School Count

Once you have narrowed down your interests and have a fairly strong idea what type of career you want to pursue, you naturally want to start putting your career path plan into motion as quickly as you can. If you are a high school student, you may feel there isn't much you can do toward achieving your career goals—other than, of course, earning good grades and graduating. But there are actually many ways you can make your high school years count toward your career in journalism before you have earned your high school diploma. This section will cover how you can use this period of your education and life to better prepare you for your career goal and to ensure you keep your passion alive while improving your skill set.

Even while still in high school, there are many ways you can begin working toward your career goal. Classes in another language, in writing, and in government or health can all help you prepare for a career as a journalist.
DGLIMAGES/ISTOCK/GETTY IMAGES.

COURSES TO TAKE IN HIGH SCHOOL

Depending on your high school and what courses you have access to, there are many subjects that will help you prepare for a career in media and journalism. To start, if your school has a newspaper (online or in print) or blog, definitely earn your bylines there. Volunteer to work on the yearbook staff as an editor or photographer, proofreader, or caption writer.

If you go to a school that offers media and journalism courses, of course that's a good place to start as well. However, there are other courses and subjects that are just as relevant to a media and journalism career. Some of them may seem unrelated initially, but they will all help you prepare yourself and develop key skills.

- *Language arts.* You can't write, edit, communicate, or edit well without strong knowledge of language arts. It won't hurt to know how to diagram a sentence or properly place a semicolon beyond a shadow of a doubt.

- *Math.* Even though you probably fancy yourself a word person, you need to be sharp in both words and numbers. Research requires an understanding of math, how to interpret statistics and percentages, and to put them into terms a viewer, reader, or listener will understand.
- *Interpersonal communications/public speaking.* These courses will be an asset in any profession but especially in media and journalism. Reporting live on the air, interviewing people on the red carpet, or even conducting a phone interview will require you to have excellent verbal communication and interpersonal communication skills.
- *Business and economics.* A lot of the news and issues around the world have to do with business and economics, so this is important to have some level of knowledge in. And as with any type of business, if you have the ambition to run your own, knowledge gained in business and economics classes will prepare you to make smarter business and financial decisions.
- *Optimization.* One of the key differences between online journalism and traditional print outlets is how a publication draws its audience. These days, ranking high on search engines is essential to drawing traffic (that is, an audience). Search engine optimization (SEO) prowess is definitely a must.

GAINING WORK EXPERIENCE

The best way to learn anything is to do it. When it comes to preparing for a career in media and journalism, there are several options for gaining real-world experience and for getting a feel for whether you are choosing the right career for you.

The one big benefit of jobs in this industry is you don't have to land an opportunity at an established publication, for example, to prove what you've got and what you can do. Rather than wait for someone to invite you to work for them, you are wise to keep working on your own and to show not only your talent but also your passion.

This means you should do it on your own and create a strong portfolio. Your strongest writing samples—the more relevant to journalism the better, of course— should be featured in your portfolio or your best photojournalism work if that is your ambition. Or both, because many publications now seek out professionals who are both writers and photographers. If you are interested in broadcasting, put together samples of your best video or audio work. And remember, even if this work has not commissioned by anyone and is something you've worked on in your spare time, share it if it is of the quality you want to project.

HOW TO CREATE A PODCAST

If you have broadcast ambitions, starting a podcast is a great way to flex your writing, interviewing, and speaking muscles.

A podcast, in essence, is an audio broadcast that can be recorded and shared online. Some are free and some require subscription. There is a podcast for nearly everything these days, from crime-solving serials (such as the aptly named *Serial* podcast) to subjects from cooking to business to foreign language learning. There is probably a podcast on anything you can imagine. Some are produced by celebrities, but many are created by people who are passionate about a topic and want to share a message.

The popularity of podcasts in the United States took a sharp rise in recent years. In 2019, the *New York Times* reported that "more than half the people in the United States have listened to one, and nearly one out of three people listen to at least one podcast every month. Last year, it was more like one in four."[2] Here are some other impressive stats:[3]

- In 2006, only 22 percent of consumers knew what a podcast was, but by 2019 more than 64 percent of consumers were aware of podcasting.
- Seventy percent of Americans are familiar with podcasting, and 50 percent of the US population have listened to a podcast. In 2019, 32 percent, or ninety million Americans, listened to a podcast in the last thirty days.
- By 2022, it's estimated that podcast listening will grow to 132 million people in the United States.

Of course, with all this growing popularity, there are many podcasts out there competing for listeners' ears: an estimated 850,000 worldwide.[4] Before you begin drafting a script or lining up guest interviews (if you plan to do either—it's your show, after all) think about your concept: What's your topic, your audience, your style? A podcast about music may be too broad as a description, but if you are particularly interested in say, heavy metal on the ukulele (look it up, it's a thing), then you've got a pretty niche concept.

Understand your goals. Is you podcast intended to educate? To entertain? To give you a platform to share your opinion on current events? Will it be focused on you, or will you interview or include others? Is it fun or serious? Will you draft scripts, have "guests," or just talk off the cuff?

Covering all the technical requirements and steps to recording and editing a podcast is beyond the scope of this book, but search online where you will find a wealth of information, tips, and advice on how to produce a high-quality podcast without spending a lot money or having to learn complicated software.

Here are the basic steps to planning and recording a podcast:

1. Pick your topic and make it as unique and defined as you can. Don't be too general or vague.
2. Name your podcast something that will draw your audience. Think about the design and music you will create for it. Although you don't want to get too stuck on this before considering the actual content, thinking about this may help you further conceptualize the audience you want to attract and image you want to portray.
3. Choose a podcast hosting provider. There are many, such as Bluehost and HostGator. You can also make podcasts on applications you may already have, such as Spotify. Some are free, and some charge a free; do some research and pick one that has the features you need at a cost that you can cover.
4. Record your podcast. The best part of podcasting is you don't need a sophisticated studio to do it. Get a USB microphone, and you're ready for business.
5. Edit each segment (many podcasts are "broadcast" in 20- to 45-minute segments or episodes) so it's ready to share. You'll used audio-editing software for this.
6. Get the word out! Share your work via social media and get your friends and family to do the same to build an audience.

Sometimes our best work is that which comes from a genuine interest and passion rather than something we are paid to do. Your portfolio is your best shot to show who you really are as a reporter, writer, broadcaster, and so on, as well as what types of stories interest you and how creative you are in "telling" them.

HOW TO START CREATING AN ATTENTION-GRABBING ONLINE WRITING PORTFOLIO

Throughout your career as a writer, you will be asked to share your work. It makes sense: Although your résumé and educational background may showcase a lot of your achievements and qualifications for a job or an assignment in journalism, what really speaks best for you and your skills is your actual work.

And as mentioned previously: If you don't have much or even any professional work—meaning, work you've been assigned from an editor at a publication, online or off—you can still show your skills by sharing writing you've done for your own purposes and interest, such as blog posts.

There are many online tools that can help you prepare your portfolio, with which you can share your best work to date by sharing one link, as opposed to submitting several links to different articles or, worse, file attachments.

The online tools, many of which are available free but some of which are not, take you through the steps of creating a site that showcases your work and lets you share a little bit about who you are and how to reach you. As always online, be careful what personal details you share online! Some sites give you the option to be reached by viewers only through your site, which is preferable to giving your personal email address. But it is not necessary to share this information at all; in most cases, you will use your portfolio to reach out to editors and not the other way around.

Some sites to check out:

- Clippings.me (https://www.clippings.me)
- Journo Portfolio (https://www.journoportfolio.com)
- Contently (https://contently.com)
- WordPress (wordpress.com)
- Muck Rack (https://muckrack.com/journalists)

NOTE: In the world of media and journalism, for better or worse, your social media presence is a factor for when you are looking for assignments or jobs. If you have a large following on Twitter, for example, that indicates to potential employers that you are someone who already has an audience built in, which bodes well for any articles you publish. Remain professional on social media, however, because anything you post—our own work, opinion, jokes, things you've forwarded—will also be accessible to potential employers. So although social media is an excellent if not necessary tool for journalists, it should be used professionally—and, of course, safely.

Keeping things offline, it's also a good idea to arrange to shadow a professional in the field, in whichever capacity you find most interesting to you. This means accompanying someone to work, observing the tasks performed, the work culture, the environment, the hours, and the intensity of the work. Talk with people you know who work in the media or journalism business. Read and watch interviews with journalists and media professionals you admire.

Educational Requirements

Whatever type of job you want to pursue in media and journalism, you should expect to have to earn at minimum a four-year bachelor's degree. In other cases a master's or even a doctorate degree is recommended. In addition there are certificate programs you can earn at your community college or online to continue or broaden your education throughout your career. Thomas Foundation (http://www.thomsonfoundation.org) offers a variety of professional development courses for people working in journalism and media, for example.

USEFUL NONJOURNALISM COURSES TO FOLLOW

Although a degree in something directly related to your goal, be it journalism, mass communications, technology, or film or television studies, will definitely help you get on track to the career of your dreams, there are other courses to consider that will help you succeed once your work life is launched in the media and journalism industry. If you want to be a book or journal editor, news editor, reporter, broadcaster, or what have you, with a particular specialization, you should consider staying abreast of your focus of interest. Here are just some examples of subjects you can start taking classes in (at any point in your education career):

- *Business classes.* Business knowledge comes in handy in many ways for a journalist. You may have the ambition to work for a magazine or section of a newspaper that focuses on business news. Or perhaps you have more entrepreneurial ambitions and want to start your own news site or publication.
- *Finance/economics courses.* These are relevant for similar reasons as business classes. If you want to focus your journalistic and media know-how on

finance issues—or again, want to start your own publication—you should definitely learn about finance and economics.

- *Health care/science.* Again, many jobs in media and journalism that focus on health care, and other scientific topics will require at least some background in that area.
- *Interpersonal communications.* Interviewing is a key aspect of most journalists' jobs, and that requires being the type of communicator people trust, feel safe talking with, and want to share their stories with. It's also a crucial skill to have in any profession that requires teamwork.
- *A second (or third) language.* To broaden your scope in every way, fluency in another language is valuable. It will help you in your research, in uncovering stories, interviewing sources, and should you desire a life as a foreign correspondent.
- *Creative writing.* Sure, it's not nonfiction writing, but the more you can learn about effective, elegant style in writing, the better your writing will be across the board, from a long-form feature in the *New Yorker* to your emails to colleagues.
- *Politics/government/international relations.* You can't cover global issues, governments, the White House, and so on, without a working knowledge of and interest in politics and international relations.

Later in this chapter, we will discuss the considerations to keep in mind when deciding what level of education is best for you to pursue. In chapter 3, we will outline in more detail the types of programs offered and the best schools to consider, should you want to pursue training and certification after high school or an associate's, bachelor's, or master's degree.

"When it all gets too much, I just step away, have a good cry, talk with my wife or one of my sisters, drink wine, eat chocolate, get a massage, schedule therapy. Then I get back to it. Even when I want to quit, I know I can't. I'm a writer. It's how I process what's happening in my life and in the world."—Annie L. Scholl, writer and journalist

WHY CHOOSE AN ASSOCIATE'S DEGREE?

A two-year degree—called an associate's degree—is sufficient to give you a knowledge base to begin your career and can form as a basis should you decide to pursue a four-year degree later. Do keep in mind, though, that media and journalism jobs are quite competitive. If you are prepared to put in the financial and time commitment to earn an associate's degree and are sure of the career goal you have set for yourself, consider earning a bachelor's instead. With so much competition out there, the more of an edge you can give yourself, the better your chances will be.

WHY CHOOSE A BACHELOR'S DEGREE?

A bachelor's degree—which usually takes four years to earn—is a requirement in most cases for a career in media and journalism, and even if one can sell an article to a publication without showing proof of a degree, to work full-time as a journalist or media professional you should expect to need a bachelor's degree. And in general, the more education you pursue, the better your odds are to advance in your career, which means more opportunity and often, more compensation. (As well as contacts, work samples, and experience, etc.)

The difference between an associate's and a bachelor's degree is of course the amount of time each takes to complete. To earn a bachelor's degree, a candidate must complete forty college credits, compared with twenty for an associate's. This translates to more courses completed and a deeper exploration of degree content, even though similar content is covered in both.

> Even when not required, a master's degree can help advance your career, give you an edge over the competition in the field, and give you more specific knowledge relating to your work in the media and journalism industry.

WHY CHOOSE A MASTER'S DEGREE?

A master's degree is an advanced degree that usually takes two years to complete. A master's will offer you a chance to become more specialized and to build on the education and knowledge you gained while earning your bachelor's.

A master's can be done directly after your bachelor's, although many people choose to work for a while in between to discover what type of master's degree is most relevant to their careers and interests. Many people also earn their master's degree while working full- or part-time.

In some instances, a doctorate degree will be required, depending on your career goals. To be an editor in chief at an academic publisher, a doctorate is often required in the subject matter, for example. If you have the desire to teach at the university level—in journalism or communications, for instance—you will be required to hold a doctorate in a relevant subject.

COMBINING LOVE FOR PUBLISHING WITH A PERSONAL PASSION

C. B. is an equine journalist who writes about the care, management, behavior, and physiology of horses. A military brat, She grew up in Europe, riding horses in every country her father was stationed in. She received her British Horse Society teaching certification when she was seventeen. After graduating from the University of Maryland with a degree in journalism, she was able to combine her two interests to become an equine journalist. She began working at a magazine as an intern in 1994, has spent her entire career with the publication and currently serves as managing editor.

Why did you choose to become a journalist?
I have always enjoyed writing, both creative and expository. My favorite school assignments always involved writing, and I worked on the school newspaper. I was a prolific letter writer back before emails and texts and Snapchats were a thing. My original career plan wasn't journalism, though. I started out wanting to work in the equestrian world as a trainer or instructor or barn manager. When it became clear that wasn't going to be a long-term good fit for me, I fell back on what I knew I would like doing—writing. Journalism offered the most flexibility in

terms of career paths, and I was ultimately able to combine my passion for horses with my love of writing.

What is a typical day on the job for you?

The typical day depends on what phase of magazine production we are in. In the early days of the cycle, I'm brainstorming ideas, interviewing sources, and writing stories. As layout begins, I'm looking for suitable photographs and writing captions. Then we have days of proofreading, then final checks to get the pages to the printer on time. It's a predictable cycle, but each day in the process is a little different. In between all of the magazine work, I'm doing digital projects, tending to social media, creating podcasts, and doing other tasks, but print deadlines are immobile, so they dictate the overall workflow.

What's the best part of your job?

I get paid to be curious and nosy. Some of my favorite stories I've written started out as a question that dawned on me while riding, or a single line in a research paper that intrigued me. I didn't have to wonder what it meant, though. . . . I just looked up the correct expert and sent an email. I guess anyone could technically do that—most experts are thrilled to be asked about their work—but I get paid to write down and share their answers with a community I feel connected to. That's the best part.

What's the worst or most challenging part of your job?

The shifting nature of the industry. Journalism has to continually change to survive, but staying true to the fundamentals of good writing and serving your core audience while navigating "reinventions" and "pivots" on the business side is crucial. Keeping your mission in focus amid turmoil can be tough.

What's the most surprising thing about your job?

It's not glamorous. Many people think I get to ride and play with horses all day then write up my personal reflections like some sort of horsey Carrie Bradshaw. It's not like that at all. There's a lot of grunt work, like proofreading and fact-checking and sending emails to people you hope reply quickly. The writing is an important part, but only one part, of the entire job.

What kinds of qualities do you think one needs to be successful at this job?

You need many qualities that may seem to be at odds with each other: Very organized but flexible. Tenacious but polite. Focused but nimble. Adaptable but resilient. Open-minded but mission-focused.

How do you combat burnout?

I combat burnout by making sure there are hours in a day and days in the week when I simply don't work. You've got to meet deadlines, but you've also got to be able to disconnect. I just close the computer and go do something else. That takes more discipline than you'd think.

What would you tell a young person who is thinking about becoming a journalist?

Don't do it for money or job security or a stress-free lifestyle. Really, the only reason to do it is because you care deeply about and feel very connected to the audience you'll be serving.

—————

Summary

This chapter covered a lot of ground in terms of how to break down the challenge of not only discovering what career within the media and journalism industry is right for you and in what environment, capacity, and work culture you want to work but also how best to prepare yourself for achieving your career goal.

In this chapter, you learned about the broad range of roles that fall under the career umbrella of the media and journalism industry. And although the various careers that exist—from editor in chief to photojournalist—the chapter also pointed to many tools and methods that can help you navigate the confusing path to choosing a career that is right for you. It also addressed some of the specific training and educational options and requirements and expectations that will put you, no matter what your current education level or age, at a strong advantage in a competitive field.

Use this chapter as a guideline for how to best discover what type of career will be the right fit for you and consider what steps you can already be taking to get there. Some tips to leave you with:

- Take time to carefully consider what kind of work environment you see yourself working in and what kind of schedule, interaction with colleagues, work culture, and responsibilities you want to have.

- Follow the news—not just the stories, but trends in writing styles, interview formats, production techniques (for television and radio), new and innovative news sites, publications, and broadcasts. Be aware of how technology is used and what new technologies exist.
- Equally, keep up with the actual news. If you want to follow a certain subject matter, be it show ponies or astrophysics, read, listen to, and watch as much as you can about your area of interest.
- Start immediately keeping a portfolio of you work. If you don't have any professional work to highlight, you can still show off your skills to potential employers or schools. Write, record podcasts, make videos, take photographs—whatever format you choose.
- Shadow a professional to get a feeling for the hours kept, challenges faced, and the overall job. Find out what education or training he or she completed.
- Investigate various colleges and certification options so you can better prepare yourself for the next step in your career path. (More on this in chapter 3.)
- Don't feel you have to wait until you graduate from high school to begin taking steps to accomplish your career goals. You can already begin by working on your portfolio so you can showcase your artwork, for example.
- Keep work-life balance in mind. The career you choose will be one of many adult decisions you make, and ensuring that you keep all of your priorities—family, location, work schedule—in mind will help you choose the right career for you, which will make you a happier person.

The next chapter details the next steps—writing a résumé and cover letter, interviewing well, follow-up communications, and more. This is information you can use to secure internships, volunteer positions, summer jobs, and more. It's not just for college grads. In fact, the sooner you can hone these skills, the better off you'll be in the professional world.

3

Pursuing the Educational Path

Making decisions about your educational path can be just as daunting as choosing a career path. It is a decision that not only demands understanding what kind of education or training is required for the career you want but also what kind of school or college you want to attend. There is a lot to consider no matter what area of study you want to pursue and depending on the type of job you want to have within the journalism and media field.

Now that you've gotten an overview of the different degree and certificate options that can prepare you for your future career, this chapter will dig more deeply into how to best choose the right type of study for you. Even if you are years away from earning your high school diploma or equivalent, it's never too soon to start weighing your options, thinking about the application process, and of course, taking time to really consider what kind of educational track and environment will suit you best.

Some people choose to start their careers right away after graduating with a high school degree or equivalent. If you are seeking work as a freelance journalist, for example, you will not be asked to present a degree. But if you are seeking full-time employment at an established news or media company, it will be required. And in any case, attending a college or university will provide you the opportunity to hone your writing and grammatical skills, receive feedback from instructors who have worked in the field, and gain work experience as you write for school- or internship-related publications, sites, or news organizations.

Not everyone wants to take time to go to college or pursue other forms of academic-based training. But if you are interested in following the educational path—from earning a certificate in writing or editing to a four-year university degree—this chapter will help you navigate the process of deciding on the type of institution you would most thrive in, determining what type of degree you want to earn, and looking into costs and how to find help in meeting them.

The chapter will also give you advice on the application process, how to prepare for any entrance exams such as the SAT or ACT that you may need to take, and how to communicate your passion, ambition, and personal experience in a personal statement. When you've completed this chapter, you should have a good sense of what kind of education after high school is right for you and how to ensure you have the best chance of being accepted at the institution of your choice.

Finding a Program or School That Fits Your Personality

Before we get into the details of good schools for each profession, it's a good idea for you to take some time to consider what "type" of school will be best for you. Just as with your future work environment, understanding how you best learn, what type of atmosphere best fits your personality, and how and where you are most likely to succeed will play a major part in how happy you will be with your choice. This section will provide some thinking points to help you refine what kind of school or program is the best fit for you.

Note this list does not assume you intend to attend a four-year college program or complete a certification program; some of the questions may therefore be more relevant to you, depending on the path of study you mean to follow.

If nothing else, answering questions like the following ones can help you narrow your search and focus on a smaller sampling of choices. Write your answers to these questions down somewhere where you can refer to them often, such as in your notes app on your phone:

- *Size:* Does the size of the school matter to you? Colleges and universities range from sizes of five hundred or fewer students to twenty-five thousand students. If you are considering college or university, think about what size of class you would like and what the right instructor-to-student ratio is for you.
- *Community location:* Would you prefer to be in a rural area, a small town, a suburban area, or a large city? How important is the location of the school in the larger world to you? Is the flexibility of an online

degree or certification program attractive to you, or do you prefer more on-site, hands-on instruction?

- *Length of study:* How many months or years do you want to put into your education before you start working professionally?
- *Housing options:* If applicable, what kind of housing would you prefer? Dorms, off-campus apartments, and private homes are all common options.
- *Student body:* How would you like the student body to "look"? Think about coed versus all-male and all-female settings, as well as the level of diversity, how many students are part-time versus full-time, and the percentage of commuter students.
- *Academic environment:* Consider which majors are offered and at which levels of degree. Research the student-to-faculty ratio. Are the classes taught often by actual professors or more often by the teaching assistants? Find out how many internships the school typically provides to students. Are independent study or study abroad programs available in your area of interest?
- *Financial aid availability/cost:* Does the school provide ample opportunities for scholarships, grants, work-study programs, and the like? Does cost play a role in your options? (For most people, it does).
- *Support services:* Investigate the strength of the academic and career placement counseling services of the school.
- *Social activities and athletics:* Does the school offer clubs that you are interested in? Which sports are offered? Are scholarships available?
- *Specialized programs:* Does the school offer honors programs or programs for veterans or students with disabilities or special needs?

Not all of these questions are going to be important to you, and that's fine. Be sure to make note of aspects that don't matter so much to you too, such as size or location. You might change your mind as you go to visit colleges, but it's important to make note of where you are to begin with.

U.S. News & World Report puts it best when they say the college that fits you best is one that will do all these things:

- Offers a degree that matches your interests and needs
- Provides a style of instruction that matches the way you like to learn
- Provides a level of academic rigor to match your aptitude and preparation
- Offers a community that feels like home to you
- Values you for what you do well

MAKE THE MOST OF CAMPUS VISITS

If it's at all practical and feasible, you should visit the campuses of all the schools you're considering. To get a real feel for any college or university, you need to walk around the campus, spend some time in the common areas where students hang out, and sit in on a few classes. You can also sign up for campus tours, which are typically given by current students. This is another good way to see the campus and ask questions of someone who knows. Be sure to visit the specific school/building that covers your possible major as well. The website and brochures won't be able to convey that intangible feeling you'll get from a visit. Also, make a list of questions that are important to you before you visit.

In addition to the questions listed in the previous section in this chapter consider these following questions as well.

- What is the makeup of the current freshman class? Is the campus diverse?
- What is the meal plan like? What are the food options?
- Where do most of the students hang out between classes? (Be sure to visit this area.)
- How long does it take to walk from one end of the campus to the other?
- What types of transportation are available for students? Does campus security provide escorts to cars, dorms, and so on at night?

To be ready for your visit and make the most of it, consider these tips and words of advice.

Before you go:

- Be sure to do some research. At the least, spend some time on the college website. Make sure your questions aren't addressed adequately there first.
- Make a list of questions.
- Arrange to meet with a professor in your area of interest or to visit the specific school.

- Be prepared to answer questions about yourself and why you are interested in this school.
- Dress in neat, clean, and casual clothes. Avoid overly wrinkled clothing or anything with stains.
- Listen and take notes.
- Don't interrupt.
- Be positive and energetic.
- Make eye contact when someone speaks directly to you.
- Ask questions.
- Thank people for their time.

Finally, be sure to send thank-you notes or emails after the visit is over. Remind the recipient when you visited the campus and thank them for their time.

Hopefully, this section has impressed upon you the importance of finding the right fit for your chosen learning institution. Take some time to paint a mental picture of the kind of university or school setting that will best complement your needs. Then read on for specifics about each degree.

In the academic world, accreditation matters and is something you should consider when choosing a school. Accreditation is basically a seal of approval that schools promote to let prospective students feel sure the institution will provide a quality education that is worth the investment and will help graduates reach their career goals. Future employers will want to see that the program you completed has such a seal of quality, so it's something to keep in mind when choosing a school.

Determining Your Education Plan

There are many options, as mentioned, when it comes to pursing an education in the journalism and media field. These include vocational schools, two-year community colleges, and four-year colleges. This section will help you select the track that is most suited to you.

CONSIDERING A GAP YEAR

Taking a year off between high school and college, often called a *gap year*, is normal, perfectly acceptable, and almost required in many countries around the world, and it is becoming increasingly acceptable in the United States as well. Particularly if you want to pursue a career as a reporter, photographer, or writer, having exposure to the world outside the classroom will help you gain perspective and experience that you can immediately apply to your future work. Because the cost of college has gone up dramatically, it literally pays for you to know going in what you want to study, and a gap year—well spent—can do lots to help you answer that question. It can also give you an opportunity to explore different places and people to help you find a deeper sense of what you'd like to study when your gap year has ended.

Some great ways to spend your gap year include joining the Peace Corps or other organizations that offer opportunities for work experience. A gap year can help you see things from a new perspective. Consider enrolling in a mountaineering program or other gap-year-style program, backpacking across Europe or other countries on the cheap (be safe and bring a friend), find a volunteer organization that furthers a cause you believe in or that complements your career aspirations, join a Road Scholar program (see www.roadscholar.org), teach English in another country (see https://www.gooverseas.com/blog/best-countries-for-seniors-to-teach-english -abroad for more information), or work and earn money for college!

Many students will find that they get much more out of college when they have a year to mature and to experience the real world. The American Gap Year Association reports from their alumni surveys that students who take gap years show improved civic engagement, improved college graduation rates, and improved GPAs in college.

See their website at https://gapyearassociation.org/ for lots of advice and resources if you're considering a potentially life-altering experience.

Whether you are opting for a certificate program, or a two-year or four-year degree, you will find there are many choices of institutes and schools offering a variety of programs at different costs and durations (in the case of certificate programs, twelve to eighteen months is usually the average for full-time participants to complete the required course load). Because of this, it is important to narrow down the options and compare them closely.

It's a good idea to select roughly five to ten schools in a realistic location (for you) that offer the degree or certification you want to earn. If you are considering online programs, include these in your list. Of course, not every school near you or that you have an initial interest in will probably grant the degree you want of course, so narrow your choices accordingly. With that said, consider attending a university in your resident state, if possible, which will save you lots of money if you attend a state school. Private institutions don't typically discount resident student tuition costs.

Be sure you research the basic GPA and SAT or ACT requirements of each school as well. Although some community colleges do not require standardized tests for the application process, others do.

If you are planning to apply to a college or program that requires the ACT or SAT, advisers recommend that students take both the ACT and the SAT tests during their junior year (spring at the latest). You can retake these tests and use your highest score, so be sure to leave time to retake early senior year if needed. You want your best score to be available to all the schools you're applying to by January of your senior year, which will also enable them to be considered with any scholarship applications. Keep in mind these are general time lines; be sure to check the exact deadlines and calendars of the schools to which you're applying!

Once you have found five to ten schools in a realistic location for you that offer the degree or certification in question, spend some time on their websites studying the requirements for admissions. Important factors weighing on your decision of what schools to apply to should include whether you meet the requirements, your chances of getting in (but shoot high!), tuition costs and availability of scholarships and grants, location, and the school's reputation and licensure/graduation rates.

Most colleges and universities will list the average stats for the last class accepted to the program, which will give you a sense of your chances of acceptance.

The order of these characteristics will depend on your grades and test scores, your financial resources, work experience, and other personal factors. Taking everything into account, you should be able to narrow your list down to the institutes or schools that best match your educational or professional goals as well as your resources and other factors such as location and duration of study.

> "I get paid to be curious and nosy. Some of my favorite stories I've written started out as a question that dawned on me while riding, or a single line in a research paper that intrigued me. I didn't have to wonder what it meant, though. . . . I just looked up the correct expert and sent an email. . . . I get paid to write down and share their answers with a community I feel connected to."—C. B.

Schools to Consider When Pursuing a Career in Journalism and Media

Some schools and programs have stronger reputations than others. Although you can certainly have a successful and satisfying career and experience without going to the number one school in your field of study, it is a good idea to shop around, to compare different schools, and to get a sense of what they offer and what features of each are the most important—or least—to you.

Keep in mind there what is great for one person may not be as great for someone else. What might be a perfect school for you might be too difficult, too expensive, or not rigorous enough for someone else. Keep in mind the advice of the previous sections when deciding what you really need in a school.

GREAT SCHOOLS FOR JOURNALISM AND MEDIA

CollegeFactual.com[1] has compiled a list of the top twenty-five schools for journalism in 2020. The list is based on factors such as percentage of degree completion, educational resources available, student body caliber, and post-graduation earnings for the school as a whole. Other factors include:

- *Major focus*: How much a school focuses on journalism students compared with other majors.
- *Major popularity*: How many other journalism students choose this school.
- *Accreditation*: Whether a school is regionally accredited or a recognized journalism related accrediting body.

The top ten programs, according to this research, are listed here, from number one to number ten.

- Emerson College, Boston, Massachusetts
- University of Texas at Austin
- University of Missouri, Columbia
- Northwestern University, Evanston, Illinois
- New York University
- Boston University, Boston, Massachusetts
- University of Maryland, College Park
- University of Southern California, Los Angeles
- George Washington University, Washington, DC
- Syracuse University, New York

Should you want to pursue a master's degree or higher, many of these schools also offer such programs.

If you search for the best *communications* schools, when includes a wider range of journalism and media majors, you will get a different list than the one shown here, so don't limit your searches to just journalism.

GREAT SCHOOLS FOR PHOTOGRAPHY

If you are ready to commit yourself to a photography career, there are many bachelor's programs in the United States (as well as masters/master of fine arts programs should you choose to continue your education after earning your undergraduate degree).

Here are the top ten programs, according to their list, from number one to number ten:

- New York University
- Judson University, Elgin, Illinois
- University of Central Florida, Orlando, Florida
- Purdue University, West Lafayette, Indiana
- Marlboro College, Marlboro, Vermont
- Washington University, St. Louis, Missouri
- Freed-Hardeman University, Henderson, Tennessee
- Drexel University, Philadelphia, Pennsylvania
- Brigham Young University, Provo, Utah
- Appalachian State University, Boone, North Carolina

GREAT SCHOOLS FOR CREATIVE WRITING

If you are eager to launch your career as a writer, you should consider earning a degree that will hone your creative writing skills and understanding of the elements of good narratives. There are many master's of fine arts programs in the United States that focus on creative writing, including fiction or script writing, but as an undergrad you might consider an English literature degree and take as many creative writing courses as you can along the way. Or you might choose to focus more intently on creative writing by attending one of the following schools offering undergraduate (bachelor's) programs in creative writing.

This list—from number one to number ten—has been compiled by the Koppelman Group.[2]

- Columbia University, New York, New York
- Emory University, Atlanta, Georgia
- Washington University, St. Louis, Missouri
- Princeton University, Princeton, New Jersey
- Middlebury College, Middlebury, Vermont
- Emerson College, Boston, Massachusetts
- Cornell University, Ithaca, New York
- Hamilton College, Clinton, New York
- Bucknell University, Lewisburg, Pennsylvania
- Kenyon College, Gambier, Ohio

What's It Going to Cost You?

So, the bottom line—what will your education end up costing you? Of course that depends on many factors, including the type and length of degree or certification, where you attend (in-state or not, private or public institution), how much in scholarships or financial aid you're able to obtain, your family or personal income, and many other factors.

School can be an expensive investment, but there are many ways to seek help paying for your education.
ZIMMYTWS/ISTOCK/GETTY IMAGES.

Generally speaking, there is about a 3 percent annual increase in tuition and associated costs to attend college. In other words, if you are expecting to attend college two years after this data was collected, you need to add approximately 6 percent to these numbers. Keep in mind this assumes no financial aid or scholarships of any kind.

WRITING A GREAT PERSONAL STATEMENT FOR ADMISSION

The personal statement you include with your application to college is extremely important, especially when your GPA and SAT/ACT scores are on the border of what is typically accepted. Write something that is thoughtful and conveys your understanding of the profession you are interested in, as well as your desire to practice in this field. Why are you uniquely qualified? Why are you a good fit for this university? These essays should be highly personal (the "personal" in personal statement). Will the admissions professionals who read it, along with hundreds of others, come away with a snapshot of who you really are and what you are passionate about?

Look online for some examples of good ones, which will give you a feel for what works. Be sure to check your specific school for length guidelines, format requirements, and any other guidelines they expect you to follow.

And of course, be sure to proofread it several times and ask a professional (such as your school writing center or your local library services) to proofread it as well.

Financial Aid: Finding Money for Education

Finding the money to attend college, whether is two or four years, an online program, or a vocational career college can seem overwhelming. But you can do it if you have a plan before you actually start applying to college. If you get into your top-choice university, don't let the sticker cost turn you away. Financial aid can come from many different sources, and it's available to cover all different kinds of costs you'll encounter during your years in college, including tuition, fees, books, housing, and food.

The good news is that universities more often offer incentive or tuition discount aid to encourage students to attend. The market is often more competitive in favor of the student, and colleges and universities are responding by offering more generous aid packages to a wider range of students than they used to. Here are some basic tips and pointers about the financial aid process:

- You apply for financial aid during your senior year of high school. You must fill out the Free Application for Federal Student Aid (FAFSA)[3] form, which can be filed starting October 1 of your senior year until June of the year you graduate. Because the amount of available aid is limited, it's best to apply as soon as you possibly can. See fafsa.gov to get started.

- Be sure to compare and contrast deals you get at different schools. There is room to negotiate with universities. The first offer for aid may not be the best you'll get.
- Wait until you receive all offers from your top schools and then use this information to negotiate with your top choice to see if they will match or beat the best aid package you received.
- To be eligible to keep and maintain your financial aid package, you must meet certain grade/GPA requirements. Be sure you are clear on these academic expectations and keep up with them.
- You must reapply for federal aid every year.

Watch out for scholarship scams! You should never be asked to pay to submit the FAFSA form (*free* is in its name) or be required to pay a lot to find appropriate aid and scholarships. These are free services. If an organization promises you that you'll get aid or that you have to "act now or miss out," these are both warning signs of a less-reputable organization.

Also, be careful with your personal information to avoid identity theft as well. Simple things like closing and exiting your browser after visiting sites where you entered personal information (like fafsa.gov) goes a long way. Don't share your student aid identification number with anyone either.

It's important to understand the different forms of financial aid that are available to you. That way, you'll know how to apply for different kinds and get the best financial aid package that fits your needs and strengths. The two main categories that financial aid falls under is *gift aid*, which doesn't have to be repaid, and *self-help aid*, which are either loans that must be repaid or work-study funds that are earned. The next sections cover the various types of financial aid that fit in one of these areas.

GRANTS

Grants typically are awarded to students who have financial needs but can also be used in the areas of athletics, academics, demographics, veteran support, and special talents. They do not have to be paid back. Grants can come from federal agencies, state agencies, specific universities, and private organizations. Most federal and state grants are based on financial need.

Examples of grants are the Pell Grant, SMART Grant, and the Federal Supplemental Educational Opportunity Grant (FSEOG). Visit the US Department of Education's Federal Student Aid site for lots of current information about grants (see https://studentaid.ed.gov/types/grants-scholarships).

SCHOLARSHIPS

Scholarships are merit-based aid that does not have to be paid back. They are typically awarded based on academic excellence or some other special talent, such as music or art. Scholarships also fall under the areas of athletic-based, minority-based, aid for women, and so forth. These are typically not awarded by federal or state governments but instead come from the specific university you applied to as well as private and nonprofit organizations.

Be sure to reach out directly to the financial aid officers of the schools you want to attend. These people are great contacts who can lead you to many more sources of scholarships and financial aid. Visit http://www.gocollege.com /financial-aid/scholarships/types/ for lots more information about how scholarships in general work.

LOANS

Many types of loans are available especially to students to pay for their postsecondary education. However, the important thing to remember here is that loans must be paid back with interest. Be sure you understand the interest rate you will be charged. This is the extra cost of borrowing the money and is usually a percentage of the amount you borrow. Is this fixed or will it change over time? Is the loan and interest deferred until you graduate (meaning you don't have to begin paying it off until after you graduate)? Is the loan subsidized (meaning the federal government pays the interest until you graduate)? These are all points you need to be clear about before you sign on the dotted line.

There are many types of loans offered to students, including need-based loans, non-need-based loans, state loans, and private loans. Two reputable federal loans are the Perkins Loan and the Direct Stafford Loan. For more information about student loans, start at https://bigfuture.collegeboard.org /pay-for-college/loans/types-of-college-loans.

FEDERAL WORK-STUDY

The US federal work-study program provides part-time jobs for undergraduate and graduate students with financial need so they can earn money to pay for educational expenses. The focus of such work is on community service work and work related to a student's course of study. Not all colleges and universities participate in this program, so be sure to check with the school financial aid office if this is something you are counting on. The sooner you apply, the more likely you will get the job you desire and be able to benefit from the program, because funds are limited. See https://studentaid.ed.gov/sa/types/work-study for more information about this opportunity.

THE HIGH-PRESSURE DEMANDS OF BROADCAST NEWS

Fiona Kelly, originally from Northern Ireland, graduated from the University of Wales Aberystwyth in 2002 with a degree in film and television studies. She moved to the Netherlands, and in 2007 started her editing career with an entry position at a Dutch broadcasting company where she has now worked for thirteen years. Beginning as a junior editor, she is now a senior editor and mainly focuses on national and Dutch entertainment news.

Fiona Kelly
COURTESY OF FIONA KELLY.

Why did you choose to become a video editor in news broadcasting?

That was very roundabout. Believe it or not, but I had always wanted to be a medical doctor, a pediatrician as it happens. (Let's not blame Dr. Ross and *ER* for this, and yes, that is my era—he only helped me decide on my specialty.) Anyway as so often happens, a young impressionable teenager is impressed by a young "trendy" teacher who happened to teach drama. I decided to broaden my horizons and took up drama. When applying for university, I needed to further expand on this and added film and TV as my minor. After my first year at university, I dropped the theater altogether. More and more of my chosen modules were practical based, and I really focused on editing and studio work. Then after another random blip where I moved to the Netherlands and learned a new language and went down many side paths of working in flower bulb factories, postal companies, and pubs and restaurants, I applied for a "grown-up" job. I knew very little about the whole process in the Netherlands, but eventually got accepted as a junior editor for the postproduction department of a Dutch news company, and I haven't looked back since. What is interesting is that originally I never saw myself working in news. I was always more focused on fiction, really wanting to work in film, but life is funny like that, you mold to changes and it's amazing how a person can adapt and thrive wherever we end up. I can't really imagine doing anything else now.

What is a typical day on the job for you?

I usually start at 3 p.m. and which shift I'm doing totally determines how my day goes. We have several broadcast deadlines per day: late afternoon, early evening and a late edition. Although sometimes if current events allow, this can change. I could be responsible for making sure all newly filmed material is correctly loaded into the system for the reporters to edit for their news stories, I could be working on the final edits of the news items, when I need to make sure the news stories are complete and sent on time for broadcast, or I could be the video coordinator, one of my favorite shifts (though also the one that causes me the most stress), where I need to make sure all the news stories are picked up by an editor and sent on time, I am the direct line with the production control room and need to keep them aware of any problems or changes. In a live broadcast situation, this can be a high-stress position, but thankfully our setup at work means that we switch between various roles during the week.

What's the best part of your job?

The variety. The news itself is forever changing. I need to be able to switch from a regular day to days where it seems like the world has turned upside down in an unforeseen, sudden way. I work with a fabulous team, and it is quite amazing how we can all pull together and make sure, whatever is thrown at us, that we can get it on air so that the viewer can follow important events as they unfold, and be informed as to how it could affect them.

What's the worst or most challenging part of your job?

The switch of tempo can make me crazy sometimes, but it's also what gets the adrenaline flowing. If it has been very quiet for a while, with no "new" news, we can almost fall into a rut. It's almost rhythmic, then we really need to switch up a gear if something unexpected happens, then I really need to give myself a shake and just get on with it. Also outside the day-to-day news, our department is constantly evolving with technology, and that keeps me on my toes. If I think back to when I started and all the footage was physically delivered on tape for us to digitize, now everything is a lot more immediate and we can get material on air from source to the studio within seconds if needed.

What's the most surprising thing about your job?
The team. I had never expected how close we would become.

What kinds of qualities do you think one needs to be successful at this job?
I have worked with people who have been trained up right from school to college or university and worked with someone who joined our team after working as a tram driver. The one thing that has connected them all is a willingness to learn and adapt. Technology is constantly making advances. I need to be able to not only roll with the changes but to embrace them and figure out how they work to my advantage. Also and not less important is to be able to say you don't understand something. With such tight deadlines (mere seconds sometimes), we have no time for mistakes, so if you come up against something at any stage that you don't understand or can't do, you need to speak up and ask how to do it so that when you need that knowledge you have it. If mistakes are made, and we are only human, after all, you need to own them and do everything you can do to not let them happen again. Recognizing mistakes works preventatively. If you can see them coming, you can fend them off. The ability to make yourself clear in a short space of time is crucial. You would be surprised by how often problems come down to simply errors in communication. And, last but not least, the ultimate cliché—multitasking. Editing can be very tunnel-visioned work, but with news, everything needs done at once, there is usually very little time for changes or second versions. Is the footage good, is the sound clear, does it have the correct levels, is the voice track in the correct place, is it broadcastable? There isn't always time for multiple viewings. Being able to check all that and make quick decisions in one go is crucial.

How do you combat burnout?
Even though we have very "high-pressure" deadlines as we make multiple live news programs per day, the switching up of the shifts really helps. I'm not always responsible for the whole lineup, and even when I am, we have a great team, so I know if there is an issue my colleagues have my back. I think it is important that we are all in the same boat and tend to look out for each other. Yes, I have crazy shifts, but with the right team and knowing when to let of steam, it isn't an issue. Also I crochet, and it's a great wind down, funnily enough since starting to crochet I have gone as far as learning to technically edit crochet patterns. Totally different meaning of the word edit, though (ha ha). Winding down for me now includes not only testing and editing patterns, but designing my own, making clothes and writing my blog *Kelly's*

Krochet. It seems like even more work and pressure, but it is so different it doesn't feel like that to me. It is the same for any career. You need to have outside interests or hobbies to help switch off.

What would you tell a young person who is thinking about becoming a video editor in news broadcasting?
If it is what interests you and you have the opportunity to do so, I would definitely recommend following a course or gaining some type of associated qualification if you can. Know what work you are applying for is also a must. So many times I have been in interviews where candidates didn't know what they had applied for, or what was expected from them. They saw it as a possible springboard into "the media." Trust me, editing isn't one of the glamour roles. Once you have had a start don't get complacent. Keep abreast of technical developments, be prepared for changes, be flexible in your approach. The way the news is made and delivered is constantly changing, and our tools as editors are also. It is easy to get left behind. Don't let that happen.

Summary

This chapter covered all the aspects of college and postsecondary schooling or certification that you'll want to consider as you move forward. Remember that finding the right fit is especially important, because it increases the chances that you'll stay in school and earn your degree or certificate, as well as have an amazing experience while you're at it. The careers covered in this book have varying educational requirements, which means that finding the right school or program can be different depending on your career aspirations.

In this chapter, we discussed how to evaluate and compare your options to get the best education for the best deal. You also learned a little about scholarships and financial aid, how the SAT and ACT tests work, if applicable, and how to write a unique personal statement that eloquently expresses your passions.

Use this chapter as a jumping-off point to dig deeper into your particular area of interest. Some tidbits of wisdom to leave you with:

- Take the SAT and ACT tests early in your junior year so you have time to take them again. Most universities automatically accept the highest scores.
- Make sure that the institution you plan to attend has an accredited program in your field of study. Some professions follow national accreditation policies, whereas others are state-mandated and, therefore, differ across state lines. Do your research and understand the differences.
- Don't underestimate how important campus visits are, especially in the pursuit of finding the right academic fit. Come prepared to ask questions not addressed on the school website or in the literature.
- Your personal statement is an important piece of your application that can set you apart from others. Take the time and energy needed to make it unique and compelling.
- Don't assume you can't afford a school based on the "sticker price." Many schools offer great scholarships and aid to qualified students. It doesn't hurt to apply. This advice especially applies to minorities, veterans, and students with disabilities.
- Don't lose sight of the fact that it's important pursue a career that you enjoy, are good at, and are passionate about! You'll be a happier person if you do so.

At this point, your career goals and aspirations should be gelling. At the least, you should have a plan for finding out more information. Remember to do the research about the university, school, degree, or certificate program before you reach out and especially before you visit. Faculty and staff find students who ask challenging questions much more impressive than those who ask questions that can be answered by spending ten minutes on the school website.

In the next chapter, we go into detail about the next steps—writing a résumé and cover letter, interviewing well, follow-up communications, and more. This is information you can use to secure internships, volunteer positions, summer jobs, and more. It's not just for college grads. In fact, the sooner you can hone these communication skills, the better off you'll be in the professional world.

4

Writing Your Résumé and Interviewing

You are now well on your way to mapping your path to achieve your career goals in media and journalism. With each chapter of this book, we have narrowed the process from the broadest of strokes—what is meant by media and journalism, what kinds of jobs exist in the industry, and to how to plan your strategy and educational approach to making your dream job a reality.

In this chapter, we will cover the steps involved in applying for jobs or schools: how to prepare an effective résumé and slam-dunk an interview. Your résumé is your opportunity to summarize your experience, training, education, and goals and attract employers or school administrators. The goal of the résumé is to land the interview, and the goal of the interview is to land the job. Even if you do not have much working experience, you can still put together a résumé that expresses your interests and goals and the activities that illustrate your competence and interest.

As well as a résumé, you will be expected to write a cover letter that is basically your opportunity to reveal a little bit more about your passion, your motivation for a particular job or educational opportunity, and to express more about you personally to give a potential employer a sense of who you are and what drives you. And particularly because you are striving for a career in a competitive and creative field—as well as one that requires a passion for current events and storytelling—you want to be sure that what makes you uniquely suited for an opportunity comes through.

Giving the right impression is undoubtedly important, but don't let that make you nervous. In a résumé, cover letter, or interview, you want to put forward your best but your genuine self. Dress professionally, proofread your résumé and writing samples carefully ahead of time, and ensure you are being and coming across as yourself. Particularly in media, projecting your own voice and point of view is key.

In this chapter, we will cover all of these important aspects of the job-hunting process and by the end you will feel confident and ready to present yourself as a candidate for the job you really want.

Writing Your Résumé

Writing your first résumé, or one early in your career, can feel challenging because you have likely not yet gained a lot of experience in a professional setting. But don't fret: Employers understand that you are new to the workforce or to the particular career you are seeking. The right approach is never to exaggerate or invent experience or accomplishments but to present yourself as someone with a good work ethic, a genuine interest in the particular job or organization, and a natural talent for communication and ability to seek out a good story to tell and use what you can to present yourself authentically and honestly.

There are some standard elements of an effective résumé that you should be sure to include. At the top should be your name, of course, as well as email address or other contact information. Always list your experience in reverse chronological order, beginning with your current or most recent position—or whatever experience you want to share. If you are a recent graduate with little work experience, begin with your education. If you've been in the working world for a while, you can opt to list your education or any certification you have at the end. If you are transitioning to journalism and media from a different career, be sure and explain your reasons and highlight what previous work experience is relevant and will strengthen your abilities in a new field. For example, if you worked in education or law and come with experience in a particular field, you will appeal to publications focusing on these areas.

Be sure you include any volunteer or other community service work you have done, and list any publications in which your work has been featured (keeping in mind you will more than likely also be submitting writing samples). Writing samples need not be published by a professional news outlet or organization. Many writers who display their talents via personal blogs go on to land paying gigs at prime publications.

The important thing is to present the most important and relevant information at the top. With only six seconds to make an impression, your résumé needs to be easy to navigate and read.

Before you even begin to write your résumé, do your research. Make sure you get a good sense of what kind of candidate or applicant a school or an employer is looking for. You want to not only come across as competent and qualified but also want to seem like just the right fit for just that job within that organization or publication. Familiarize yourself with their work, staff you may be familiar with and admire (editor, writers, radio hosts, and so on), the focus of their work (subject matter, mission, political affiliation), writing style, audience, and anything else that shows you are interested in what they do because it matches what you can and want to do.

You may need to customize your résumé for different purposes to ensure you are not filling it with information that does not directly link to your qualifications for a particular job.

You can then begin to make a list of all the relevant experience and education you have. Highlight your education where you can—any courses you've taken, be it in high school or through a community college or any other place that offers training related to your job target. Also highlight any hobbies or volunteer experience you have—again, only as it relates to the job you are after.

Your résumé is a document that sums up who you are and indicates in what ways you will be an asset to your future employer. It should also be concise: One page is usually appropriate, especially for your first résumé.

Before preparing your résumé, try to connect with a hiring professional—a human resources person or hiring manager—in a similar position or organization you are interested in. They can give you advice on what employees look for and what information to highlight on your résumé, as well as what types of interview questions you can expect. If you know anybody working in journalism and media, it's a good idea to ask for advice or perhaps have a look at their résumé to learn more about what works in the industry.

As important as your résumé's content is the way you design and format it, especially for a job in media and journalism. You can find several samples online of résumés that you can be inspired by. At TheBalanceCareers.com,[1] for example, you can find many templates and design ideas. You want your résumé to be attractive to the eye and formatted in a way that makes the key points easy to spot and digest; according to some research, employees take an average of six seconds to review a résumé, so you don't have a lot of time to get across your experience and value.

LINKING-IN WITH IMPACT

As well as your paper or electronic résumé, creating a LinkedIn profile is a good way to highlight your experience and promote yourself, as well as to network. Joining professional organizations or connecting with other people in your desired field are good ways to keep abreast of changes and trends and work opportunities.

The key elements of a LinkedIn profile are your photo, your headline, and your profile summary. These are the most revealing parts of the profile and the ones employers and connections will base their impression of you on.

The photo should be carefully chosen. Remember that LinkedIn is not Facebook or Instagram; it is not the place to share a photo of you acting too casually on vacation or at a party. According to Joshua Waldman, author of *Job Searching with Social Media For Dummies*,[2] the choice of photo should be taken seriously and be done right. His tips:

- Choose a photo in which you have a nice smile.
- Dress in professional clothing.
- Ensure the background of the photo is pleasing to the eye. According to Waldman, some colors—like green and blue—convey a feeling of trust and stability.
- Remember it's not a mug shot. You can be creative with the angle of your photo rather than stare directly into the camera.
- Use your photo to convey some aspect of your personality.
- Focus on your face. Remember visitors to your profile will see only a small thumbnail image, so be sure your face takes up most of it.

Your headline will appear just below your name and should summarize—in 120 characters—who you are, what you do, what you are interested in doing, and what you are motivated by. Take your time with this; it is your opportunity to sell yourself in a brief and impactful manner. Related but separate is your summary section. Here, you can share a little more about yourself than in your headline, but it should still be brief. Waldman recommends your summary take no more than thirty seconds to read aloud (so, yes, time yourself!) and that it be short (between five and ten lines or three to five sentences), concise, and unique, and that it tell a story.

WRITING AN OBJECTIVE

The objective section of your résumé is one of the most important, because it is the first section a recruiter or hiring manager will read and, therefore, the first sense they will develop of you as a candidate. The objective should be brief and to the point. Definitely it should be focused and give a sense of you as a unique applicant; you don't want it to be generic or bland. It's important to take your time and really refine your objective so you can stand out and attract employers or clients.

At BestRésuméExamples.com,[3] you can find a lot of solid advice about how to write an objective for a journalism and media résumé, such as ensuring you carefully read the job description so you know exactly what kind of journalist, writer, editor, and so on the organization is looking for. Then you can better craft your objective to highlight the ways in which you uniquely match their needs.

Here are some examples offered at BestRésuméExamples.com:

"A self-motivated and highly organized unique storyteller seeks the position of Multimedia Journalist at XXY Inc. Bringing excellent communication skills, both verbal and written, two years' experience working in a multimedia environment, and the ability to apply Sony EX3 and DSLR cameras to shoot and deliver promotable and compelling stories, in contributing top quality content to the company's website and social media platforms."

"A talented journalist with five years' writing and copy editing experience in the broadcast media desires the job of Senior Writer at XYZ Media where effective communication and leadership skills, as well as strong desire to mentor aspiring journalists will be utilized in leading the company's Show team."

"To obtain the job of Journalism Partnerships Manager at XYZ Inc. to provide quality leadership to the News Partnership team that collaborates with journalists for news gathering. Coming with seven years News media, project, and people management experience, as well as exceptional ability to think critically and strategically about issues and come up with useful recommendations and effective plan of action."

"A young talented individual pursuing a Bachelor's Degree at XYZ State University, with passion for news and the Internet desires to join the team at XYZ News Inc. as Digital Journalism Intern to be able to have a well-rounded newsroom education as well as a portfolio of forty to sixty articles. Possess strong web news writing skills and experience working with campus newspaper."

"A highly experienced multi-platform editor, digitally aware, skilled with words, and endowed with the ability to work effective under deadline pressure, seeks to join the team at XYZ News Service as Copy Editor. Coming with a track record of delivery high level of clarity, accuracy, and balance in copy editing functions."

"I love the independence of writing—just me and the keyboard, typing away. I love creating an online community around my words. I love the challenge of capturing the nuance of something ephemeral or complicated. . . . When I am successful, I feel accomplished, productive, relevant, connected. The connection with readers is probably the best part of blogging. It is still surprising and humbling that strangers on the Internet take the time to read what I write and seem to care about what I have to say."—Sheila Quirke, freelance blogger and writer

Writing Your Cover Letter

As well as your résumé, most employers will ask that you submit a cover letter. This is a one-page letter in which you express your motivation, why you are interested in the organization or position, and what skills you possess that make you the right fit.

Here are some tips for writing an effective cover letter:

- As always, proofread your text carefully before submitting it. This is important in any job field but particularly if you are submitting yourself as a candidate for a job in writing and editing.
- Be sure you have a letter that is focused on a specific job. Do not make it too general or one-size-fits-all. Your personality and uniqueness should come through, or the recruiter or hiring manager will move on to the next application. Again, particularly for a career in journalism or media, your writing style and "voice" will be important in helping you stand out from the competition.
- Summarize why you are right for the position. Keep it relevant and specific to what the particular publication or organization is looking for in a candidate and employee.
- Keep your letter to one page whenever possible.
- Introduce yourself in a way that makes the reader want to know more about you, and encourage them to review your résumé.
- Be specific about the job you are applying for. Mention the title and be sure it is correct.
- Try to find the name of the person who will receive your letter rather than keeping it nonspecific ("to whom it may concern").
- Be sure you include your contact details.
- End with a "call to action"—a request for an interview, for example.

Interviewing Skills

With your sparkling résumé and LinkedIn profile, you are bound to be called for an interview. This is an important stage to reach: You will have already gone through several filters—a potential employer has gotten a quick scan of your experience and has reviewed your LinkedIn profile and has made the decision to learn more about you in person.

> "I have photographed A-list celebrities and professional sports and news events that have changed the lives of so many. Creating those photographs was exciting but also devastating, and I believe they are important historical records."—Robin Barrett, photojournalist

There's no way to know ahead of time exactly what to expect in an interview, but there are many ways to prepare yourself. You can start by learning more about the person who will be interviewing you. In the same way recruiters and employers can learn about you online, you can do the same. You can see if you have any education or work experience in common, or any contacts you both know. It's perfectly acceptable and even considered proactive in a positive way to research the person with whom you'll be interviewing, such as on LinkedIn.

Naturally, a job interview can be stressful. You can help calm your nerves and feel more confident if you prepare ahead by thinking about answers to questions you can anticipate being asked.
ANDREYPOPOV/ISTOCK/GETTY IMAGES.

Preparing yourself for the types of questions you will be asked to ensure you offer a thoughtful and meaningful response is vital to interview success. Consider your answers carefully, and be prepared to support them with examples and anecdotes.

Depending on the position to which you are applying, you may be asked to do an editing or writing "test" as part of the interview process. This can entail editing an article according to house style as well as the standard rules of grammar, spelling, and punctuation or writing a short article in a set amount of time. There's no real way to prepare for this except to know to expect it. The test will be designed to ensure you can perform at the quality level necessary and in a timely manner, under pressure. Just breathe and do your best.

Here are some questions you should be prepared to be asked. It's a good idea to consider your answers carefully, without memorizing what you mean to say (because that can throw you off and will be obvious to the interviewer). Think carefully about your responses and be prepared to deliver them in a natural manner.

- Why did you decide to enter this field? What drives your passion for working within the media and journalism industry?
- What is your educational background? What credentials did you earn?
- What publishing experience do you have as an editor or writer?
- Are you a regular reader, listener, or viewer of our work, and if so what do you like about it? What might you want to make different?
- What did you like best about the education experience? What did you like least?
- Are you a team player? Describe your usual role in a team-centered work environment. Do you easily assume a leadership role?

BEWARE WHAT YOU SHARE ON SOCIAL MEDIA

Most of us engage in social media. And for writers and journalists, it's pretty much a necessity for building an audience and having a platform to share your writing skills, point of view, and give a sense of what news and stories you find most important.

Sites such as Facebook, Twitter, and Instagram provide us a platform for sharing photos and memories, opinions, and life events and reveal everything from our political stance to our sense of humor. It's a great way to connect with people around the world, but once you post something, it's accessible to anyone—including potential employers—unless you take mindful precaution.

Your posts may be public, which means you may be making the wrong impression without realizing it. More and more, people are using search engines like Google to get a sense of potential employers, colleagues, or employees, and the impression you make online can have a strong impact on how you are perceived. According to CareerBuilder.com,[4] 60 percent of employers search for information on candidates on social media sites.

Glassdoor.com[5] offers the following tips for how to avoid your social media activity from sabotaging your career success:

1. Check your privacy settings. Ensure that your photos and posts are only accessible to the friends or contacts you want to see them. You want to come across as professional and reliable.

2. Rather than avoid social media while searching for a job, use it to your advantage. Especially as a journalist or media job applicant, it's to your advantage to have an online presence (as long as it's a flattering one). Give future employees a sense of your professional interest by "liking" pages or joining groups of professional organizations related to your career goals.

3. Grammar counts. Be attentive to the quality of writing of all your posts and comments.

4. Be consistent. With each social media outlet, there is a different focus and tone of what you are communicating. LinkedIn is professional, whereas Facebook is far more social and relaxed. It's okay to take a different tone on various social media sites, but be sure you aren't blatantly contradicting yourself.

5. Choose your username carefully. Remember, social media may be the first impression anyone has of you in the professional realm.

Dressing Appropriately

How you dress for a job interview is important to the impression you want to make. Remember that the interview, no matter what the actual environment in which you'd be working, is your chance to present your most professional self. Although you will not likely ever wear a suit to work, for the interview it's the most professional choice. Keep in mind also, depending on the nature of the job to which you are applying, in many journalism and media jobs you will likely be representing your place of employment in the public, so the way you come across is important.

Although you may be applying for a job in a casual environment or working in the field, until the job is yours it's important to come across as a professional, including dressing the part when you interview. A suit is no longer an absolute requirement, but avoid looking too casual, because it will give the impression you are not that interested.

What Employers Expect

Hiring managers and human resource professionals will also have certain expectations of you at an interview. The main thing is preparation: It cannot be overstated that you should arrive to an interview appropriately dressed, on time, unhurried, and ready to answer—and ask—questions.

For any job interview, the main things employers will look for are that you

- Have a thorough understanding of the organization and the job for which you are applying
- Be prepared to answer questions about yourself and your relevant experience
- Be poised and likeable but still professional. They will be looking for a sense of what it would be like to work with you on a daily basis and how your presence would fit in the culture of the business
- Stay engaged. Listen carefully to what is being asked and offer thoughtful but concise answers. Don't blurt out answers you've memorized; really focus on what is being asked.
- Be prepared to ask your own questions. It shows how much you understand the flow of an organization or workplace and how you will contribute to it.

Some questions you can ask:

- What created the need to fill this position? Is it a new position or has someone left the organization?
- Where does this position fit in the overall hierarchy of the organization?
- What are the key skills required to succeed in this job?
- What challenges might I expect to face within the first six months on the job?

- How does this position relate to the achievement of the company's (or department's or boss's) goals?
- How would you describe the organization's culture?

HAVE A THICK SKIN AND KEEP ON WRITING

Annie L. Scholl got her bachelor's in journalism and mass communication from the University of Iowa in 1985. She worked as a newspaper reporter for about fifteen years, the bulk of that time at the *Cedar Rapids Gazette* in her hometown. She worked in marketing for about ten years before starting Annie Scholl Creative in 2010. Annie was a full-time freelance writer for another ten years before taking a full-time position as a senior content writer for a higher education marketing firm.

Annie L. Scholl
COURTESY OF ANNIE L. SCHOLL.

Annie, who is at work on a memoir, blogs at *anniescholl.com* and contributes to *Huffington Post* as a guest writer. She also writes regularly for *Unity Magazine*, *Daily Word*, and the *Sunlight Press*. Her work has been published by *Brevity* and *Past Ten* as well as other online outlets. She lives in North Carolina with her wife Michelle and their two dogs and three cats.

Why did you choose to become a writer?

In fourth grade, I wrote a story sparked by an experience with my two little sisters. I asked my art teacher if she would do the illustrations for it. She did. I remember stapling an orange construction paper cover on it. Maybe it all started there.

When I graduated from high school, my plan was to become an English teacher like my beloved teacher Carolyn Taylor. I went to the University of Northern Iowa, what was known then as a teachers' college, and I was miserable. I decided to transfer to the University of Iowa because it was closer to home. When I was going through the course catalog I found the BA in Journalism and Mass Communication. I knew instantly that's what I wanted to do. I earned my degree in four years, graduated, and went right to work for a small daily in northwest Iowa. I was a general assignment reporter there and quickly learned hard news reporting wasn't for me. I worked as a feature writer at the *Green Bay Press-Gazette* for about a year before moving back to my hometown to take a job at the *Cedar Rapids Gazette*. I left daily newspaper writing in December 2000. For the past twenty years, I've primarily worked as a higher education marketing writer, but I also still freelance and am at work on a memoir.

What is a typical day like for you?

I meditate every morning. Any personal writing—work on my memoir, a blog post—I'll do in the morning, because it's my best time to write. Most days my wife and I walk our dogs and then have coffee together on our back deck. I then dive into my work as a senior content writer for a higher education marketing company. Most of my days are spent writing web pages, landing pages, social media ads, and messaging and persona documents. I've been taking a writing class and working one-on-one with my teacher to finish my memoir so a couple evenings a week are dedicated to that.

What's the best part of your job?

Telling stories and making connections. In August 2020, a devastating derecho (a hurricane-like storm) hit my beloved Iowa. While my family and friends were dealing with no power and the destruction to their homes and properties, I was in North Carolina a thousand miles away feeling helpless. The only way I could think of to help was to write, to bring attention to a story the national media had largely ignored. I wrote a piece that was published on *Huffington Post*. I also wrote a blog for my personal website (anniescholl.com). Both were widely read and shared. Yes, plenty of internet trolls had hateful things to say, but I heard from dozens who thanked me for writing, who said I expressed what they were feeling. Knowing that something I wrote helped someone or moved someone—to tears, laughter, or action—is why I love being a writer. Even in my work as a marketing writer, I'm trying to make an emotional connection with the reader. I also love seeing my words come to life in a web page design or a magazine article. I still get a kick out of that after thirty-five years.

What's the worst or most challenging part of your job?

Being misunderstood. You write something, and you put it out in the world, and you have no control over how it's received or perceived. You know what your intention was when you wrote it, but people can only read through their own lens. My skin is mighty thick after three and a half decades as a writer, but the criticism can still sting. I also battle crippling self-doubt at times where I just want to hang it up as a writer. That's not true in my marketing work—I feel very confident in that arena—but it does come into play in my personal writing. I try and shift out of that place of fear, that place of ego, and instead focus on being of service—of writing something that someone, somewhere needs to hear.

What's the most surprising thing about your job?
Sometimes I'm amazed at what comes up when I write. I'll read back over something and think, wow, where did that come from? It's not of my conscious creation. When I allow the writing to come from my heart versus my head, that's when I do my best work. In my work as a marketing writer, what surprises me is how much I still have to learn. Marketing is continually evolving, particularly writing for the Web. I've been doing this work since 2002 and I'm still learning. That's what I love about it, too.

What kinds of qualities do you think one needs to be successful at this job?
Curiosity. Compassion. Perseverance. A thick skin. An open heart. A willingness to put yourself out there and be vulnerable. A willingness to take what comes in the form of criticism without taking it personally or internalizing it. As a marketing writer, you have to be curious and know how to ask questions and listen to answers so that you can emotionally connect with consumers. With that said, I couldn't market something I don't believe in, so writing for higher ed is an ideal fit for me. I like helping people find the right college or university where they can learn what they need to learn to bring their dreams to life.

How do you combat stress and burnout?
I definitely felt burned out when I was writing daily for a newspaper. I was primarily writing personality profiles, and while I loved interviewing people and sharing their stories, cranking out a half-dozen or more each week made me feel like a factory worker. I do get stressed with my marketing work—I have a lot on my plate and constant deadlines to meet—but the truth is I do my best work under pressure. I wish I didn't, but I do. When it all gets too much, I just step away, have a good cry, talk with my wife or one of my sisters, drink wine, eat chocolate, get a massage, schedule therapy. Then I get back to it. Even when I want to quit, I know I can't. I'm a writer. It's how I process what's happening in my life and in the world.

What would you tell a young person who is thinking about becoming a writer?
When I was in journalism school, I had to write a piece and then share it with my source. He tore it apart, and I was devastated. I went crying to my professor, and he told me if I couldn't handle criticism, I best pick a different career. I knew this was mine to do, so I wasn't going to quit—despite being a sensitive person. You

do have to have a thick skin as a writer. You are going to be misunderstood. You are going to be criticized. Editors are going to critique your work. You have to be willing to write and rewrite. But when you write something and it lands on somebody, when what you wrote made them laugh or cry—or when they say, "Thank you for putting words to what I've been feeling," well, it really doesn't get any better.

If you want to write, write. Don't give in to the negative voices, particularly your own. Be willing to work at your craft. Read and write. Take classes and workshops. Keep going.

Summary

Congratulations on working through the book! You should now have a strong idea of your career goals within the media and journalism field and how to realize them. In this chapter, we covered how to present yourself as the right candidate to a potential employer, and these strategies are also relevant if you are applying to a college or another form of training.

Here are some tips to sum it up:

- Your résumé should be concise and focused on only relevant aspects of your work experience or education. Although you can include some personal hobbies or details, they should be related to the job and your qualifications for it.
- Take your time with all your professional documents—your résumé, your cover letter, your LinkedIn profile—and be sure to proofread carefully to avoid embarrassing and sloppy mistakes.
- Prepare yourself for an interview by anticipating the types of questions you will be asked and coming up with professional and meaningful responses.
- Equally, prepare some questions to ask your potential employer at the interview. This will show you have a good understanding and interest in the organization and what role you would have in it.
- Always follow up after an interview with a letter or an email. An email is the fastest way to express your gratitude for the interviewer's time and restate your interest in the position.

- Dress appropriately for an interview and pay extra attention to tidiness and hygiene.
- Be wary of what you share on social media sites while job searching. Most employers research candidates online, and what you have shared will influence their idea of who you are and what it would be like to work with you.

The journalism and media field is an exciting and growing one with many different types of jobs and work environments. This book has described the various jobs and provided examples of real working professionals and their impressions of what they do and how they prepared—through education or training—to do it. We hope this will further inspire you to identify your goal and know how to achieve it.

You've chosen a field that is ever-changing, in terms of how news is delivered and what technologies are used, but the role of a journalist or media professional is one that has an important societal function and offers an opportunity to expand your horizons, meet interesting and inspiring people, and keep you connected to the world and what goes on in it. It is one that will offer a fulfilling, diverse, and challenging career path that will surely broaden your worldview and ensure that you continue learning throughout your career. I wish you great success in your future.

Glossary

bachelor's degree: A four-year degree awarded by a college or university.

beat: A particular subject that a reporter is assigned to follow and deliver news about.

bias: A preset opinion or leaning that impacts how news is interpreted and delivered.

blogger: A person who produces content online for a blog, usually from his or her own perspective and based on a particular subject matter.

broadcast journalist: A journalist who produces audio or visual content for radio, Internet, or television, as opposed to print.

burnout: Feeling of physical and emotional exhaustion caused by overworking.

cable news: Cable channels that are dedicated to producing news content.

campus: The location of a school, college, or university.

career assessment test: A test that asks questions particularly geared to identify skills and interests to help inform the test taker on what type of career would suit them.

colleagues: The people with whom a person works.

columnist: A person who regularly delivers opinion-based pieces for a news publication or service.

community college: A two-year college that awards associate degrees.

copyeditor: A person who checks texts for grammar and punctuation and often writes headlines.

correspondent: A person who contributes stories to a news organization.

cover letter: A document that usually accompanies a résumé and allows candidates applying to a job or a school or internship an opportunity to describe their motivation and qualifications.

deadlines: Targets set relating to when a particular task needs to be completed. In journalism and media, deadlines are often extremely tight and change frequently.

educational background: The degrees a person has earned and schools attended.

entertainment journalism: A type of journalism that focuses on entertainment and entertainment-related news.

entrepreneur: A person who creates, launches, and manages his or her own business.

financial aid: Various means of receiving financial support for the purposes of attending school. This can be a grant or scholarship, for example.

fourth estate: A term used to define the media and its role in society.

freelancer: A person who owns their own business through which he or she provides services for a variety of clients.

gap year: A year between high school and higher education or employment during which a person can explore his or her passions and interests, often while traveling.

General Education Development (GED) degree: A degree earned that is the equivalent to a high school diploma without graduating from high school.

industry: The people and activities involved in one type of business, such as the business of the media.

internship: A work experience opportunity that lasts for a set period of time and can be paid or unpaid.

interpersonal skills: The ability to communicate and interact with other people in an effective manner.

interviewing: A part of the job-seeking process in which a candidate meets with a potential employer, usually face-to-face, to discuss work experience and education and seek information about the position.

job market: A market in which employers search for employees and potential employees search for jobs.

major: The subject or course of study in which a person chooses to earn a degree.

master's degree: A degree that is sought by those who have already earned a bachelor's degree to further their education.

networking: The processes of building, strengthening, and maintaining professional relationships as a way to further career goals.

online journalism: A type of journalism that is available online as opposed to in print.

on-the-job training: A type of training in which a person is learning while actually doing the job in a real-world environment.

photojournalist: A journalist who tells stories with photography as opposed to words.

podcast: An audio program available online that can be news-based or focused on any topic.

portfolio: A collection of work, be it writing, animation, or any other form of creative output, that represents the talents and abilities of the artist.

Pulitzer Prize: A prestigious prize awarded for the highest-quality journalism.

résumé: A document, usually one page, that outlines a person's professional experience and education and is designed to give potential employers a sense of a candidate's qualifications.

social media: Websites and applications that enable users to create and share content online for networking and social-sharing purposes. Examples include Facebook and Instagram.

source: A person who informs a journalist about a story, offering insight and information.

sports journalism: A type of journalism focused on sports and sports-related news.

style sheet: A document that outlines conventions particular to a publication or news service, which can include anything from how certain terms are used to how capitalization is used in headlines.

tuition: The money charged by an institution offering a university degree or a certification.

twenty-four-hour news: A news service—either radio, Internet, or television—that produces news twenty-four hours a day.

work culture: A concept that defines the beliefs, philosophy, thought processes, and attitudes of employees in a particular organization.

Notes

Introduction

1. Bureau of Labor Statistics, "Career as a Journalist: Job Duties and Employment Outlook," accessed April 24, 2020, https://study.com/career_as_a_journalist.html.

2. Market Watch, "The Rise of 'Fake News' Is Producing a Record Number of Journalism Majors," accessed April 24, 2020, https://www.marketwatch.com/story/the-rise-of-fake-news-is-producing-a-record-number-of-journalism-majors-2018-03-19.

3. Fit Small Business, "Best Cities for Journalists 2019: Newspaper, TV & Radio," accessed April 24, 2020, https://fitsmallbusiness.com/best-cities-for-journalists/.

Chapter 1

1. Indeed.com, "9 Types of Journalism to Explore," accessed April 29, 2020, https://www.indeed.com/career-advice/career-development/types-of-journalism.

2. Brookings.edu, "Ten Noteworthy Moments in U.S. Investigative Journalism," accessed April 29, 2020, https://www.brookings.edu/blog/brookings-now/2014/10/20/ten-noteworthy-moments-in-u-s-investigative-journalism/.

3. Bureau of Labor Statistics, "Career as a Journalist."

4. Market Watch, "The Rise of 'Fake News' Is Producing a Record Number of Journalism Majors," accessed April 24, 2020, https://www.marketwatch.com/story/the-rise-of-fake-news-is-producing-a-record-number-of-journalism-majors-2018-03-19.

5. Study.com, "Editor-in-Chief," accessed April 29, 2020, https://study.com/articles/Job_Description_of_an_Editor-in-Chief.html.

6. Bureau of Labor Statistics, "Editor," accessed April 29, 2020, https://www.bls.gov/ooh/media-and-communication/editors.htm.

7. Bureau of Labor Statistics, "Editor," accessed April 29, 2020.

8. Bureau of Labor Statistics, "Editor," accessed April 29, 2020.

9. Bureau of Labor Statistics, "Reporters, Correspondents, and Broadcast News Analysts," accessed April 29, 2020, https://www.bls.gov/ooh/media-and-communication/reporters-correspondents-and-broadcast-news-analysts.htm#tab-3.

10. Bureau of Labor Statistics, "Reporters, Correspondents, and Broadcast News Analysts."

11. Bureau of Labor Statistics, "Reporters, Correspondents, and Broadcast News Analysts."

12. Bureau of Labor Statistics, "Photographers," Accessed April 29, 2020. https:// www.bls.gov/ooh/media-and-communication/photographers.htm.

13. Bureau of Labor Statistics, "Reporters, Correspondents, and Broadcast News Analysts."

14. Bureau of Labor Statistics, "Reporters, Correspondents, and Broadcast News Analysts."

Chapter 2

1. https://www.washington.edu/doit/preparing-career-online-tutorial.

2. Jaclyn Peiser, "Podcast Growth Is Popping in the U.S., Survey Shows." *New York Times*, accessed April 30, 2020, https://www.nytimes.com/2019/03/06/business /media/podcast-growth.html.

3. Buzzsprout.com, "Podcast Statistics: Growth and Demographic Data for 2019," accessed April 30, 2020, https://www.buzzsprout.com/blog/podcast-statistics.

4. Music Oomph, "The Meteoric Rise of Podcasting: Insights about the Most Compelling Audio Format," accessed April 30, 2020, https://musicoomph.com /podcast-statistics/.

Chapter 3

1. https://www.usnews.com/education/best-colleges/right-school/choices/articles /college-personality-quiz.

2. CollegeFactual.com, "2020 Best Colleges for Journalism," https://www.college factual.com/majors/communication-journalism-media/journalism/rankings/top-ranked /?utm_expid=.v-e8XTzdRiuEkiX6YUCncQ.0&utm_referrer=https%3A %2F%2Fwww.google.com%2F.

3. https://www.koppelmangroup.com/blog/2017/11/5/the-best-under graduate-creative-writing-programs.

4. fafsa.gov.

Chapter 4

1. The Balance Careers, accessed February 11, 2020, https://www.thebalance careers.com/student-resume-examples-and-templates-2063555.

2. Joshua Waldman, *Job Searching with Social Media For Dummies* (Hoboken, NJ: Wiley and Sons, 2013).

3. BestResumeObjectives.com, "Top 10 Journalist Resume Objective Examples You Can Apply," accessed July 31, 2020, https://bestresumeobjectiveexamples.com/top -10-journalist-resume-objective-examples-you-can-apply/.

4. Career Builder, accessed February 11, 2020, http://www.careerbuilder.com /share/aboutus/pressreleasesdetail.aspx?ed=12%2F31%2F2016&id=pr945&sd =4%2F28%2F2016.

5. Alice A. M. Underwood, "9 Things to Avoid on Social Media While Looking for a New Job," accessed May 18, 2019, https://www.glassdoor.com/blog/things -to-avoid-on-social-media-job-search/.

Further Resources

The following websites, magazines, and organizations can help you further investigate and educate yourself on journalism and media-related topics, all of which will help you as you take the next steps in your career, now and throughout your professional life.

Publications

Columbia Journalism Review
cjr.org
Calling itself the "voice of journalism," this journal strives to be the intellectual leader in the changing world of journalism.

Publishing Executive
pubexec.com
A source of information about the magazine publishing industry, aimed at helping magazine publishers and editors keep up-to-date in a constantly evolving industry.

Nieman Journalism Lab
niemanlab.org
An online publications dedicated to helping journalists keep up in the Internet age of media.

Editor and Publisher
editorandpublisher.com
A print and online publication dedicated to the publishing and editing industry.

Shutter Magazine
Behindtheshutter.com
A source providing current, cutting-edge educational content for photographers, by photographers.

Blogger Magazine
http://bloggermagazine.net
An online magazine that publishes blogs on a variety of topics, including how to market yourself as a blogger. Offers inspiration for bloggers.

Professional Organizations

Society of Professional Journalists
spj.org
An organization dedicated to protecting and perpetuating free press and ensuring it maintains its role as the cornerstone of liberty in the United States.

Association of American Editorial Cartoonists
editorialcartoonists.com
An organization that is committed to promoting the interests of editorial cartoonists and political cartoonists in the United States.

Committee to Protect Journalists
cpg.org
An organization that works on behalf of journalists who are threatened by attacks, imprisonment, or other mistreatment, tracking and monitoring press freedom violations.

Fourth Estate
fourthestate.org
Fourth Estate is dedicated to ensuring the press is enabled to act as a "force of good" in society, advocating a fair and responsible free press that delivers trustworthy news.

International Women's Media Foundation
imwf.org
Offers training, fellowships, and funding among other resources to ensure women continue to have a crucial role in journalism and media.

International Federation of Journalists
ifj.org
With a membership of nearly six hundred thousand journalists worldwide, this organization works to ensure there are strong unions and fair pay, including gender equality, in the media.

Investigative Reporters and Journalists
https://ima-make-up.com
A grassroots nonprofit that creates a platform for journalists worldwide to share story ideas, news-gathering tips, and other resources. Based out of the Missouri School of Journalism, it was formed in 1973.

American Society of Media Photographers
asmp.org
The leading trade association for photojournalists. It is a leader in promoting photographers' rights, as well as providing other professional development and trade-related resources.

Bibliography

Antonoff, Steven R. "College Personality Quiz." *US News and World Report.* July 31, 2018. Accessed August 28, 2020. https://www.usnews.com/education /best-colleges/right-school/choices/articles/college-personality-quiz.

BestResumeObjectives.com. "Top 10 Journalist Resume Objective Examples You Can Apply." Accessed July 31, 2020. https://bestresumeobjectiveexam ples.com/top-10-journalist-resume-objective-examples-you-can-apply/.

Brookings.edu. "Ten Noteworthy Moments in U.S. Investigative Journalism." Accessed April 29, 2020. https://www.brookings.edu/blog/brookings-now /2014/10/20/ten-noteworthy-moments-in-u-s-investigative-journalism/.

Bureau of Labor Statics. "Career as a Journalist: Job Duties and Employment Outlook." Accessed April 24, 2020. https://study.com/career_as_a_jour nalist.html.

———. "Reporters, Correspondents, and Broadcast News Analysts." Accessed April 29, 2020. https://www.bls.gov/ooh/media-and-communication /reporters-correspondents-and-broadcast-news-analysts.htm#tab-3.

———. "Editor." Accessed April 29, 2020. https://www.bls.gov/ooh/media -and-communication/editors.htm.

———. "Photographers." Accessed April 29, 2020. https://www.bls.gov/ooh /media-and-communication/photographers.htm.

Buzzsprout.com. "Podcast Statistics: Growth and Demographic Data for 2019." April 25, 2019. Accessed April 30, 2020. https://www.buzzsprout.com /blog/podcast-statistics.

CollegeFactual.com. "2020 Best Colleges for Journalism." Accessed August 28, 2020. https://www.collegefactual.com/majors/communication-journalism -media/journalism/rankings/top-ranked/?utm_expid=.v-e8XTzdRi uEkiX6YUCncQ.0&utm_referrer=https%3A%2F%2Fwww.google .com%2F.

Fit Small Business. "Best Cities for Journalists 2019: Newspaper, TV & Radio." Accessed April 24, 2020. https://fitsmallbusiness.com/best-cities -for-journalists/.

Indeed.com. "9 Types of Journalism to Explore." Accessed April 29, 2020. https://
www.indeed.com/career-advice/career-development/types-of-journalism.

Market Watch. "The Rise of 'Fake News' is Producing a Record Number of
Journalism Majors." Accessed April 24, 2020. https://www.marketwatch
.com/story/the-rise-of-fake-news-is-producing-a-record-number-of-jour
nalism-majors-2018-03-19.

Music Oomph. "The Meteoric Rise of Podcasting: Insights about the Most
Compelling Audio Format." Accessed April 30, 2020. https://musicoomph
.com/podcast-statistics/.

Peiser, Jaclyn. "Podcast Growth Is Popping in the U.S., Survey Shows." *New
York Times*. March 6, 2019. Accessed April 30, 2020. https://www.nytimes
.com/2019/03/06/business/media/podcast-growth.html.

Study.com. "Editor-in-Chief." Accessed April 29, 2020. https://study.com
/articles/Job_Description_of_an_Editor-in-Chief.html.

About the Author

Tracy Brown Hamilton is a writer, editor, and journalist based in the Netherlands. She has written several books on topics ranging from careers to media, economics to pop culture. She lives with her husband and three children.

EDITORIAL BOARD

CPSIA information can be obtained
at www.ICGtesting.com
Printed in the USA
LVHW011717030521
686332LV00005BB/630

9 781538 144794